PRAISE FOR
BUT EVERYONE FEELS THIS WAY

"Paige Layle's book will be especially helpful to provide insight for women diagnosed with autism later in life."

—**Dr. Temple Grandin**, author of *Thinking in Pictures* and *Visual Thinking*

"Paige's heartfelt and honest account illustrates why firsthand storytelling is important for diving into the deep minds of autistic people."

—**Jory Fleming**, author of *How to Be Human. An Autistic Man's Guide to Life*

"We are in the middle of a moment of self-discovery and awakening for many Autistic adults, particularly those from marginalized backgrounds. Paige Layle's *But Everyone Feels This Way* is an important contribution to this movement, and, in its pages, I am certain many Autistics in search of understanding and a place within our growing community will see themselves."

—**Dr. Devon Price**, author of *Unmasking Autism* and *Unlearning Shame*

"I had a hard time putting this book down and the few times I did were to nod in agreement. Paige Layle writes vividly about those parts of being autistic that aren't in any psychiatry text: the constant discomfort [and] the tidal wave of emotions that overwhelm you at any moment. Paige's book offers a fuller picture of what autism looks like and, furthermore, how to build a more accepting world for Autistic people."

—**Eric Garcia**, author of *We're Not Broken: Changing the Autism Conversation*

"Paige writes with incredible insight, humor, and honesty about her autism and life. Her unique experience illustrates some universal truths, and, as I read about her, I also learned about myself and my own autism. I am grateful for the gift of her voice."

—**Kim Rhodes**, actress and activist

"Frank and perceptive, *But Everyone Feels This Way* is a welcome addition to the growing Autistic literary canon. I've long believed that Autistic voices—not a single face or voice but as many of us sharing our stories as possible—play a key role in the acceptance and celebration of Autistic people. I'm very glad that Paige's voice is among them."

—**Sarah Kurchak**, author of *I Overcame My Autism and All I Got Was This Lousy Anxiety Disorder*

"*But Everyone Feels This Way* is a poignant, brave, [and] soul-baring triumph! Whether neurotypical or divergent, Paige Layle's story will make you laugh, cry, and think. But most importantly, it will give you a new lens for seeing yourself and others."

—**Wendy Walker**, bestselling author of *American Girl*

"Genuine and heartfelt, this book will appeal to Layle's many followers on YouTube and TikTok as well as anyone seeking insight into what it means to live as a young woman navigating autism. A candid and instructive memoir about neurodivergence."

—*Kirkus Reviews*

BUT EVERYONE FEELS THIS WAY

HOW AN AUTISM DIAGNOSIS SAVED MY LIFE

PAIGE LAYLE

hachette
BOOKS

New York

Hachette Go, an imprint of Hachette Books
Hachette Book Group
1290 Avenue of the Americas
New York, NY 10104
HachetteGo.com
Facebook.com/HachetteGo
Instagram.com/HachetteGo

First Edition: March 2024

Published by Hachette Go, an imprint of Hachette Book Group, Inc. The Hachette Go name and logo are trademarks of the Hachette Book Group.

The Hachette Speakers Bureau provides a wide range of authors for speaking events. To find out more, visit hachettespeakersbureau.com or email HachetteSpeakers@hbgusa.com.

Hachette Go books may be purchased in bulk for business, educational, or promotional use. For information, please contact your local bookseller or email the Hachette Book Group Special Markets Department at Special.Markets@hbgusa.com.

The publisher is not responsible for websites (or their content) that are not owned by the publisher.

Print book interior design by Amy Quinn

Library of Congress Cataloging-in-Publication Data

Name: Layle, Paige, author.
Title: But everyone feels this way: how an autism diagnosis saved my life /
    Paige Layle.
Description: First edition. | New York: Hachette Go, 2024
Identifiers: LCCN 2023026601 | ISBN 9780306831256 (hardcover) |
    ISBN 9780306831263 (trade paperback) | ISBN 9780306831270 (ebook)
Subjects: LCSH: Autistic women. | Autistic people.
Classification: LCC HV1570.22 .L39 2024 | DDC 616.85/8820092
    [B]—dc23/eng/20231213
LC record available at https://lccn.loc.gov/2023026601

ISBNs: 9780306831256 (hardcover); 9780306831270 (ebook)

Printed in the United States of America

LSC-C

Printing 1, 2024

To all the kids out there like me. I see you.

CONTENTS

TRIGGER WARNING

This book includes discussion of suicidal ideation, a relationship between an adult and a minor, disordered eating, emotional abuse, domestic abuse, and mental illness and related hospitalization. Please read with care.

If you're in the midst of a mental health crisis, including thoughts of self-harm or suicide, call or text 988 in the United States. In Canada, call 1-833-456-4566 or text 45645.

Please note that some names and identifying characteristics have been changed. Conversations have been reconstructed.

INTRODUCTION

people have called me an educator, an advocate, and an influencer

all combined to make you

really, everything that's happened to you
in your life has made you
the person you are today; the good, the bad, the ugly
all combined to make you.
memories.
each moment in history stored
like bears store food in winter.

I HATE THE FEELING OF SWEAT ON MY SKIN. NOT JUST BECAUSE IT'S a weird liquid that oozes out of my body, and whatever comes out of my body should probably *stay away* from my body. I also *despise* being wet.

"Let's talk about Paige as a child." The psychiatrist talked down at us through a monitor, looking into the camera as he spoke, as if to give my mom and me eye contact. We sat in a small room on the end of a silent and dark hospital wing, on a floor so high up that we could see our truck low down in the parking lot if we stood by the window.

The room didn't have space for much. We sat on the only two chairs, looking up at the large monitor. There was a window to the right draped with ugly, green, patterned curtains. Mom sat in the chair closest to the window, focusing on the psychiatrist as he beamed through the screen, streaming from his office in Vancouver.

I was sweating.

"Okay," Mom said to the psychiatrist. She glanced at me, tense. "Paige can probably tell you better than I can."

"Well," he said to Mom, "I want to hear it from your perspective." A large and intimidating stuffed koala toy perched behind him, staring into my soul.

My bare legs needed to be carefully peeled off of the plastic chair; not just when it was time to stand but throughout the duration of the meeting because I didn't want to become *one* with it. I tried to create that boundary multiple times. Sitting on my hands did not prevent the stickiness from occurring but instead added a new body part that could stick too. Sweat makes everything stick to you.

I didn't find it enjoyable to have things stuck to me. My loose strands of blonde hair, once able to flow freely, clung to my temple like leeches on a host. My shirt that once felt light, almost weightless on my skin, hung heavy and close. It caught on my back as I shifted my posture.

My sweating situation was not due to the mid-August heat. The room was air-conditioned and chilled, and I'd been without physical activity for hours, waiting, talking.

I shouldn't have been sweating at all. But my brain *makes* my body hot and my skin sweat all on its own, no matter the climate. All I seemed to have to do was exist. That was—and still is—enough for my mind to race, my breathing and heart rate to increase, my legs to tense, and sweat to accumulate under my armpits (which of course increases the stickiness of my arms to my torso as well). That day, my anxiety and nerves were sky-high. My heart pounded and I shifted again in the chair. My legs bounced up and down so quickly that I vibrated. In the corner of the TV screen, I saw a reflection of myself and my beet-red face. If I were a cartoon, steam would've been coming out of my head.

"When was Paige the most happy as a baby?" the psychiatrist probed.

I turned my head to the right, my hair far too close to my neck. I pulled it all behind my shoulders. I wondered if my mom was experiencing a similar affliction and finally let myself look at her. There was no sweat along her hairline. There were no water leeches on any part of her face. I'd never even seen her sweat from stress. I couldn't tell if she had stickiness occurring on any other part of her body due to the angle at which I sat, the clothes she wore, and my fear of looking strange if I studied her body any longer than I already had.

I was being watched and analyzed, after all. It was the psychiatrist's job to figure me out. He had this one appointment to learn as much as he could, which included studying my behavior. He nitpicked and noticed every detail.

"Why did you look right at your mom like that, Paige?" the psychiatrist asked. "See how your hands are touching fingers to palms? Both of them? Why do you that with your hands, Paige?"

These were questions I could not answer.

My mom is good at talking to people, which is why she's a realtor, and she's amazing at her job. She never gets nervous or weird like I do. She can talk to hundreds of people a day, enjoy every second, and still have the energy and the care to talk to hundreds more. She doesn't need to prepare what she is going to say beforehand or plan how she is going to move her body. Words roll out of her mouth on the fly, changing to flow with the conversation.

I was so glad she was there to help me answer everything the psychiatrist wanted to know.

His questions were relentless. *He* was relentless. Nothing escaped his notice, and I could tell behind his blue glasses that he was always observing, always pondering, always accusing. It wasn't long before I became so overwhelmed and frustrated about being pummeled with questions that I struggled to speak.

"Why can't you speak?" he would ask. "Why aren't you looking at me? Why are you crying? Why are you frustrated? Why did your voice change? Why are you doing that with your hands again?"

It was as though every single action, every emotion I felt, needed to have a reason. I'm sure it did. I'm sure it does.

But I didn't know the reason.

That was why I was there: I had no answers.

I'd never had any answers, and all I wanted was answers.

The psychiatrist questioned me like I was going to say something miraculous, something informative and mind-blowing and life-changing, like he was pressing until I said the right thing that made it all click.

I didn't know why I couldn't speak. I didn't know why my eyes felt better looking at the green curtains than at his face. I didn't even notice I was doing a finger/palm thing with my hands. How could I explain *why* I did these things?

"When did Paige cry the most when she was a baby?" he asked my mom. "What toys did she like to play with? How was Paige with bedtime and bath time?"

I did not like this man.

I did not like the experience at all.

I did not like being drilled with questions I could not answer.

I did not like how he persisted despite my protest, or how he made me feel dumb for crying.

But . . . I tried really hard to cooperate as much as I could. I knew I wanted this.

We talked far longer than my social battery could withstand.

There was no specific form to fill out, no checklist the psychiatrist ticked through. There weren't even specific disorder-related questions, not for the first hour of the appointment at least. I thought I had an anxiety disorder, and perhaps obsessive-compulsive disorder (OCD). I knew that there had to be a reason why I wasn't okay, why I wasn't happy. But it wasn't disorder specific.

This was Paige specific.

This was a Paige diagnosis.

Eventually, the psychiatrist began asking more serious questions. The conversation became a trial, with my mom taking the stand, as I was too overwhelmed to answer anymore. He asked her more questions about my childhood, specifically wanting her perspective. But I interjected when her recollection was inaccurate. Due to my photographic memory, I often knew the answers better than she did. The analyst did not like the interruptions.

Mom never liked it.

I did not care. Information needed to be correct, especially today.

And then the questions stopped.

I thought the abrupt stop was because he was sick of me. I thought we were done because he didn't want to talk to me anymore. I thought we were done because I had become too difficult, and there were no other ways to formulate his questions that could make me understand and answer them properly. It was time for me to quit and give up and go home without answers. Again.

The psychiatrist leaned back in his chair and slouched ever so slightly. It was a subtle change, but it was the first time he'd moved in hours. I may not be good at deciphering the meaning behind body language, but I'm good at knowing when something's changed. He leaned back and looked at my mom and me. He was done, his conclusion made.

He waited a few silent seconds and then took a breath.

It was subtle and quick, yet it was so intense to me. I could feel his deep breath. As he inhaled, I could feel my whole world expanding, filling up like a balloon—full of thoughts, feelings, rage, confusion, suffering, hope—until my world was so full that it could not be filled anymore. There was nothing left to fit inside my world.

My world couldn't take any more things, and the power of release was his.

As he exhaled, I slowly felt everything leave me.

Hope. Confusion. Suffering.

Now, I was empty.

And then, suddenly, I filled with anticipation. All I needed to do now was wait and listen. My world only held room for that one feeling of anticipation, and it was the only thing I could do. Wait. Listen.

On that exhale, the psychiatrist released a soft sigh. Not of exhaustion, defeat, or even indifference. No, it was a sigh of discovery, a sigh of an epiphany. Like the first breath after I finished a project, stepped back from all my hard work, and finally got to enjoy the outcome without working anymore. This sigh was good. It meant he had figured something out. Heat ran down my spine with another wave of sweat. My posture shifted, mirroring what his used to display: forward leaning, offensive, ready.

I'll never forget the drastic change of his voice. His once stern and pointed tone completely vanished. He became bubbly and happy. With a slight smile, he spoke with compassion and care.

"Alright, Paige. You've done everything you need to. Now it's my turn."

answers often create more questions

a lot more people care than i thought would.
a lot more people accept me than i thought would, and it encourages me and inspires me to keep going to help more kids that were like me.
to be the person i needed when i was younger.
this book is another step.
something else that might help even just one person feel heard, seen, accepted.

For far too long, I was told I was just like everyone else. I was normal. I heard "But everyone feels this way!" as a response when I sobbed, overwhelmed by life's daily tasks.

I lived in the countryside with my mom, dad, and brother, Graham. I went to school, hung out with friends, and all the while everything seemed so much harder than it needed to be. A break in routine threw off my whole day. If my teacher couldn't answer "why" in class, I began to cry. If someone broke something important to me, I sobbed for hours. I couldn't eat any lunch other than a bologna sandwich for years. I still struggle deciding what to eat and figuring out what foods aren't going to make me want to throw up when I think about them or put them in my mouth.

My parents always said that I was okay. While everyone around me seemed to have no problem being calm and happy, I had panic attacks multiple times a day. My hyperventilating made my legs numb. Sometimes, I lost consciousness. I cried almost every day from stress, frustration, exhaustion, or all three at once.

This wasn't okay. This wasn't normal. This wasn't functioning. It certainly wasn't fine.

"You're not going to survive when you get to high school. You're not going to survive in the real world," I was told. Words that made me feel like I was a weak, selfish, terrified baby.

Early on, I didn't know that I was different from everyone else. I was told that everyone was the same as me. Everyone seemed to be doing really well, and, for some reason, I wasn't. I cried all the time, but no one seemed to take it seriously. I didn't want to cry *ever*.

People told me to stop crying, but that only made me cry more out of frustration. I didn't want anyone to know when I cried, because I didn't want anyone to yell at me for crying, so I ran and hid in a bathroom stall or my bedroom closet and tried to make myself stop.

My needs couldn't be tended to because they didn't make any sense to anyone. Especially to me.

I loved to dance: when I was a kid, it was one way that my body felt free and how I could tune out the world around me. Now, I still dance, and I teach it too. Once, at the dance studio, I arrived half an hour before class and had a panic attack. I used that time to try to calm myself down. I was panicking and hyperventilating on the dance studio floor, breathing so fast I thought I was going to die. The owner came into the studio, the laminate floors shining, the wall mirror reflecting me. She glanced over, froze as our eyes met, then turned away and started sweeping. I'm sure she didn't know what to do, but the message came to me that I was manipulative. My reasoning was: *I know that I need to comfort someone when they're upset, so maybe people don't comfort me because they don't think I'm actually upset.* Because I was like everyone else. And everyone felt this way.

Except, somewhere, deep down, I knew that wasn't true.

If everyone felt the same way I did, how come it seemed like I was the only one who didn't want to be here anymore? What was wrong with me? Living seemed so much harder for me than for everyone else.

For the first fifteen years of my life, I wondered: *What's wrong with me?*

Then I was diagnosed with autism spectrum disorder. Now I work hard to help people learn about autism on social media. Through that work I've been called an educator, an advocate, and an influencer—but initially I downloaded TikTok as a joke. I began making autism videos in March 2020 in response to a degrading post about autistic people. My platform has grown from that first post. I love connecting with people to talk about my experience and validate theirs. I'm writing this book to share my complex inner experience as a young, undiagnosed autistic child that I couldn't intellectualize then. Hopefully, by reading about my life, you find some kind of lens for your own.

There are more of us out there than you know. We remain hidden, tucked away behind corporations aiming to change us, pushing supplements and instant cures into the hands of desperate parents looking to make our lives better. We're hidden behind psychiatrists who will diagnose us with anything and everything else, because they know that people have a negative view of autism. We're hidden behind an education system that dehumanizes us and makes sure everyone else treats us like we are less than human. We're hidden behind the mask that we create ourselves to try and blend in, to not be caught.

We may act as though we're the same as you. We smile, but we dissociate when we touch a texture we don't like, or when the lights are too bright, or when we can hear every watt of electricity surging through the kitchen at night. We pretend we don't actually notice. We pretend it doesn't bother us. We try to have meltdowns and shutdowns in private to avoid being punished and ridiculed for disruptive behavior. We go through life struggling to stay afloat while it looks like everyone around us is doing just fine.

I had to hide to be safe.

We don't deserve to have to hide our whole lives and struggle in silence. We deserve inclusion, acceptance, equity, and appreciation; actually, we *need* it. We need it to survive. For many years, I struggled because I didn't know that I was autistic. The diagnosis gave me an answer.

Answers are great. Answers are helpful. But answers don't mean things change. That diagnosis gave me an avenue of hope to turn down and explore. It gave me more to learn and many new places to look for anything that could help me. My diagnosis has been a tool for me to be able to access who I really am, and it gives me the confidence and validation to say I know it for sure.

I was a lost little kid with a very complex nervous system in a world that assumed I was neurotypical. My life was filtered by layers of privilege, but I was still a really uncomfortable, unhappy, lonely kid. Being an adult gave me so much that I needed as a child, and

I'm glad that I stayed here long enough to enjoy living. This isn't a "Look, if you just do X, Y, and Z your life will get better, just like I did with mine!" book. In fact, it's very far from it. I'm not trying to give you hope either. (I hope I do, kinda, but that's not my intended purpose.) Truthfully, I share this because it pains me to think that any other kid out there feels how I felt growing up. And I want to reach them or reach someone else who can help them.

And maybe I write this because I'm still pretty young, and there's probably a small part of me that yearns for someone to hold me, tell me how my brain works, and say, "You don't have to shout so loud anymore."

No matter your reason for opening this book, thank you. I hope you turn the final page with something valuable to carry with you.

A list of my favorite things

One: I always have a notebook that I carry around everywhere. Right now, it is plain and black and has a few stickers on it. I write anything and everything in this: my thoughts and feelings, grocery lists, dance choreography . . . The point is that it's a record of my life from start to finish that I store away and can look back on. I've only begun doing this recently, because when I was younger, I segregated each "topic" into its own notebook. That led to too many notebooks.

Two: Any and all pens. My current pen twists at the tip, to retract the metal point where the ink comes out. The rotating tip is gold, much like the hardware on the opposite pole of the pen. The rest of the pen is decorated in two parts. The first half, closer to the tip, is a pale sage green. There's no pattern, but I enjoy the color. The second half of the pen is almost built like a snow globe. Picture it like this: when I shake the pen, tiny specks of gold glitter twist and twirl around bigger specks of white flowers. I hope to refill this pen with ink when it runs out, because I love it.

Three: Things for my ears. Earplugs and headphones. I have
ten pairs of earplugs that vary in noise-dampening ability, color,
and material. My Beats headphones for music are pink. I got them
for Christmas six years ago. Both are equally important for noise
control.

Four: Medium boxers from Boathouse. I sleep/lounge in them
at all times if possible. They have an impossibly comfortable fit
and material. I have eighteen pairs.

Five: Plants. I am the mother of many a plant. My baby is my
Monstera deliciosa, because it is my largest and the one I am
most excited about every time it gets a new leaf. I'm not the best
plant mom. Oftentimes it feels as though I'm just struggling to
maintain life. Everything is worth it when a new leaf pops through
the middle stem.

CHAPTER 1

WHAT WE KNOW FOR SURE ABOUT AUTISM IS VERY LITTLE

autism in girls, part 1

when doctors were studying autism,
they only studied males.
this makes it harder for anyone else
to be diagnosed because everything is based off the male
brain.
this sucks.
girls usually end up showing different traits than guys do.
which is why it can take us years to get diagnosed.

~ a random tiktok i made that got a million likes out
of nowhere

A NEURODEVELOPMENTAL DISORDER, PART ONE
Assessing ASD

Autism spectrum disorder, or ASD, is a neurodevelopmental disorder, commonly called autism, which is what I'll call it here. What we know for sure about autism is very little, but as autism is a neurodevelopmental disorder, we do know that it means that my brain developed in a different way. Autism is not a mental illness or a mental disorder or a chemical imbalance. My brain is not built the same as most people's; there's a physiological difference. I have a different category of brain. A different neurotype.

Neurological conditions are, as of now, diagnosed through behavior. A psychologist, psychiatrist, or sometimes a doctor (I don't know, a psychiatrist diagnosed me) can tell if you're autistic by just looking at how you act. They judge your behavior. They diagnose that your brain is different through your actions. All autistic people have a list of traits or behaviors that we have in common. Behaviors, like how a child plays with a car, are studied by the medical professionals to look for autistic traits.

The DSM-5 (*Diagnostic and Statistical Manual of Mental Disorders, Fifth Edition*) is a manual put together by the American Psychiatric Association that physicians commonly use all over the world to diagnose psychiatric disorders. This source has continuously been updated over the years (hence the fifth edition) to alter diagnoses as more is known about psychiatric disorders. If you google "DSM-5 autism spectrum disorder criteria," you'll see a list of what makes autism, autism (and I explore it more in the next section). Both autism and the list of behaviors are just words and ideas trying to describe a very complex inner world that some people experience, and some don't.

> I make lists all the time. Anytime I can, anytime I need to.
> I like making lists.

It's important to note that while lists are fun and helpful and useful, they don't have to be the be-all and end-all. The criteria is limited and lacks understanding of autism outside of a vacuum—or, autism in those who live with other traumas, who are socialized differently and react differently and so maybe don't exhibit the same behaviors.

Not every person will tick the exact same behavioral boxes, yet that's how someone like me gets diagnosed. In my opinion, behaviorism is an outdated science on its own because everyone responds to stimuli differently and so reacts differently. But for now, it's how things are. And what it means is that, for many neurological conditions to be diagnosed, one must be in visible *distress*, because that is when the diagnosable behaviors become most recognizable.

You don't only have a disorder when you are having a Not Good Time; you have it all the time.

False ideas about how someone "gets" autism are everywhere. These can get a lot of traction online. Sometimes truth gets lost as people try anything and everything to help their kid who has been diagnosed. Ideas float around—like that autism is caused by vaccines or autism can be cured with a specific diet—but they don't help. These false ideas can hurt autistic people.

No one "gets" autism. It's not something you can acquire. There's no "autism gene," but we've identified dozens, if not hundreds, of mutations in the genes of autistic people. We know there's a heavy genetic component (and you can't edit your genes!). If you're autistic, there's a good chance that other people in your family are too. That doesn't just go for autism but for neurodivergence in general (like attention deficit hyperactivity disorder, borderline personality disorder, OCD, anxiety, and depression). There's a high link with co-occurring conditions if you're autistic, so you may also have ADHD, intellectual disabilities, OCD, depression, anxiety, or pathological demand avoidance, for example.

Every day, neuroscience researchers learn more about autism and the physiology behind what actually makes autistic people the way we are. I hope that, with knowledge and technology continuously improving in the science world, neurologists and other experts on neurodevelopment will eventually be the ones diagnosing ASD, not psychiatrists basing their diagnosis on arbitrary actions.

A list of some of my traits

- Needing to cut all tags from my clothes
- Meltdowns if/when Mom cleaned my room
- Thinking most kids my age were dumb and boring
- Not being able to listen to fireworks, loud cars, or concerts without plugging my ears, having a meltdown, or dissociating
- Very strong sense of justice, right and wrong, fairness
- Playing with my toys by counting them and sorting them
- Sleeping with socks on
- Making up rules for myself, like every Thursday morning eat a banana, or stir your tea counterclockwise twice, then clockwise twice
- Only being interested in studying anatomy and, like, one person at a time, really intensely
- Picking at my skin, pulling out my hair
- Staring at everybody, especially while they talked
- Lots of urinary and digestive problems
- Shaking everyone's hand, regardless of age or status, when I first met them

A NEURODEVELOPMENTAL DISORDER, PART TWO

The clinical diagnosis of autism is a good, solid base of autism knowledge to start with. Now, I won't recite the DSM-5 diagnostic criteria to you, although I would love to do it by memory and show off a little. That's their book, and I'm pretty sure they want you to buy it and give them money for it and not me. Give that a separate gander for more technical terms, et cetera.

There are five key factors that must be true to conclude an autism diagnosis.

1. Persistent deficits in social communication and social interaction

2. Restrictive and repetitive patterns of behavior, interests, or activities
3. These were apparent when the person was in their early developmental years
4. Significant impairment in social, occupational, or other important areas of current function
5. These aren't better explained by an intellectual disability or global developmental delay

The first two factors are worth a bit more time here. Persistent deficits in social communication and social interaction need to be present in all three of these areas: social-emotional reciprocity (maintaining conversation, sharing interests, not being interested in other people); nonverbal communicative behaviors (abnormal body language and eye contact, not understanding facial expressions); and developing, maintaining, and understanding relationships (which speaks for itself).

But the restricted and repetitive patterns only need to be manifested in two of the following: in the body (repetitive motor movements, repeating words or phrases, lining up toys); with daily activity (distress with schedule or routine changes, same food every day); in interests (intense and abnormal fascinations with unusual interests or objects, incredibly passionate about them); or in reactions to sensory environment (hyper- or hyposensitivity to stimuli, distressed by loud noises, grumpy when wearing socks).

Conclusions I Draw

If you think you might be autistic, or you have someone in your life who is, then my first recommendation is to go to a professional. Learn as much as you can about autism while that process happens. Reading the DSM-5 definition is a good place to start, but the real-life accounts of autistic people are where you're going to get the most relatable and helpful advice. The DSM-5 doesn't describe the in-depth and painful emotions that no one other than another autistic person understands.

While you're reading the DSM-5 definition, I'd like to point out some things that can confuse people:

- Understand the context around levels of severity. You may have heard of various levels of autism, maybe 1/2/3 or that Asperger's is one "level" of autism. Levels of autism only refer to how much support the autistic person needs from someone else, with Level 1 being a little and Level 3 being a lot.

  ASD is a spectrum, and your point and your place upon it isn't identified on diagnosis.

- Notice how autism is *not* anything else. A diagnosis of an intellectual disability would have to come separately. I have many other co-occurring conditions that are not part of autism. This can be confusing for some people, who see multiple autistic people who are in fact quite different from each other, but who understand autism as only one portrayal.

  It is incredibly common for an autistic person to have co-occurring conditions that will make us different from each other.

Please Allow Me to Infodump About Neuroscience

All activity in the human body starts with tiny electrical impulses fueled by chemical fluctuations in our brain. Our brain is filled with billions of neurons that receive and send these electrical impulses to neighboring neurons, which travel down our spinal cord and to our muscles to produce an action.

The information we receive from our environment is sent to be processed in certain sections of the brain. For example, what we see is filtered through our occipital lobe, impulse control and decision-making are in the frontal lobes, and language and speech are mostly developed in the left hemisphere of the brain. The two hemispheres communicate with one another through a thick tissue called the corpus callosum, which allows information to be shared among all brain parts, even though there is specialization and lateralization.

When we're born, our brains are filled with neurons that we won't ever use. As we learn, certain pathways in our brain get stronger, and some pathways aren't touched. Simple systems become more complex as we learn, meaning we move forward with the complex system and the simple one becomes unnecessary. The neurons that aren't used go through a process called synaptic pruning. It is much more effective to drive from point A to point B on the highway than to take bumpy dirt roads that are so far off the path that the GPS can't even tell you where you are, so your brain gets rid of those confusing directions. Your brain prunes these unwieldy, unused synapses.

What you practice as a child creates strong pathways that won't be pruned away. If there are neurons in certain places that aren't utilized in a pathway—for example, if you didn't learn Spanish, how to play the guitar, or how to play soccer—those neurons that would have been used are instead not important and are taken off the GPS.

Things I learned how to do
- Sing whole musicals
- Cook Christmas dinner
- Do contemporary dance, along with hip-hop, ballet, pointe, jazz, and lyrical, but not tap
- Speak decent French
- Memorize all of the elements on the periodic table

Whether it's the learning of a skill like those, or learning how to navigate emotions like how to manage your anger, the same neuron pruning happens. It's easier to learn a new skill with lots of neurons ready to be specialized, like in early development, than it is later on.

Now here's the thing about autism: with us, this organic act of synaptic pruning doesn't happen as much as it does in allistic (non-autistic) brains. Researchers and scientists aren't sure yet why, aside from it likely being genetic. Even then, they aren't sure if this is a result of our pathways not becoming as strong, or if this is *why* our pathways don't become as strong, or if they're even related in this case.

The gist is this: we have a lot more neurons.

I never like to define people or put them in boxes, and I find metaphors challenging because of how I think about the world, but I hope carrying on with my highway analogy helps you see how neuron pruning looks.

So, when you are on the highway, you can usually drive for quite some time before getting off. Oftentimes, I can put my car in cruise control and ease down the highway for hours before I approach my exit. Highways are excellent for connecting different places that are far away and doing so in the fastest way possible. They're good for sending you along without stopping for a long time.

Allistics—people who do not have autism—have more highways in their brains. Different parts of their brain have stronger connections to each other. It's way easier for their temporal lobe to connect to the occipital, for example. The electrical pathways in their brain connect more easily, and those highways become stronger over time because the other neurons were pruned away, making that signal less interfered with. Neuron pruning shows its strength in someone without autism, because the signal is stronger and the highway is defined.

Autistic people don't have as many really strong long-term, long-distance connections or highways. This is known as long-range under-connectivity.

If you know someone who's autistic, chances are you've seen them recall seemingly unimportant events from years ago or explain every kind of dinosaur that has ever been studied or solve complicated math problems easily or know what they had for lunch three months ago on a random Tuesday. That's because the part of the brain that stores and recalls memory is just that: *one* part of the brain. We have so many neurons in a concentrated place that when that concentrated place is needed, we're very well equipped. This is called short-range over-connectivity, meaning that in short distances, our brains have a lot of connections. We're able to do single-brain-part tasks very effectively, often even more effectively than allistics. Memorization, pattern recognition, organization, picking out fine details, and sensory hypersensitivity—we have that shit on lock.

As I mentioned earlier, different parts of the brain are specialized to do certain tasks. The eyes need to send stimuli to the occipital lobe, which is at the base of your head by your neck. That information then needs to be processed elsewhere, like in your frontal lobes, which are all the way on the other side of the brain, just behind your forehead. That's, like, the farthest distance in your brain that an electrical current has to travel. So what happens when an autistic person needs multiple parts of their brain to work together?

In regard to actions like:

- Social communication
- Identifying body language
- Identifying facial expressions
- Finding the deeper meaning of texts—that is, subtexts
- Understanding abstract concepts
- Navigating social hierarchy

You may recognize these complexities as Things Autistic People Are Not Good At, but what's important about this list is that these specifically require multiple parts of the brain to work together, which requires good highway communication. There are other actions, and this list is not exhaustive. This is a general theory and doesn't cover all of what makes autistic people the way we are. Remember, too, that autistic people are not all the same. And we don't have all the same connections in the same places. I may have more neurons that control the part of my brain that deals with creative language, and someone else may have more in the mathematical area. I might be hyposensitive to taste and someone else might be hypersensitive to taste. Also, our life experiences will alter and shape us and our ways of being in the world. We are multifaceted. One of the many reasons our behaviors are different from each other and from allistic people is because of the variations in these neural connections.

A list of some of my actions, not on any DSM-5 criteria, but explained by my autism nonetheless
- Making a list of "things that someone said that people laughed at" and memorizing them to repeat at a function so everyone laughs and thinks I'm funny
- Having a really stressful time going to bed and maintaining a good sleep schedule
- Feeling love in toxic, controlling, abusive relationships
- Choosing outfits by copying someone's outfit from the day before
- Putting myself in danger or harming myself to make others comfortable
- Taking others' opinions as fact and internalizing and taking responsibility for their emotions
- Lacking true self-identity, being unable to access and therefore express my own honest feelings
- Not trusting myself or believing my own reality
- Intellectualizing emotions rather than feeling them, being unable to feel them

While all the words written in the DSM-5 mean something, autism is unique to each individual. What I love, what I value, what matters to me is what makes me, me.

A little bit more of me
- Misplacing my notebook or my pen puts me in a frenzy.
- I feel joy, I squeal, I jump up and down and sing softly to my monstera every time I see a new leaf.
- I feel gut-wrenching heartbreak at dropping a mug and cleaning up the broken shards on the ground.
- I need to alter my shower routine completely if I do not have my silicone shower hairbrush. I am not about to put my hands in my wet hair, so I need to find a new way to wash my hair.

My actions, my needs, my feelings, and my responses change over time. As we go through this book, you'll see how hard the journey was for me to get to where I am today, and how I still have a path to walk.

The other day, I was looking at photos of me as a kid. I was pretty cute, with long blonde hair, big blue eyes, and a sweet, gap-toothed smile. That smiling face held a world of complexity she couldn't understand, but I do, and in honor of all of her perseverance and hard times, I'm going to share her experiences. We'll start then, when I was just a little girl, on a quiet day just before my brother came into my life, painting Easter eggs in the kitchen.

CHAPTER 2

A HAPPY KID

a big part of growing up

becoming an adult is
understanding your trauma
and the negative experiences
that taught you wrongly

I<small>T WAS A</small> M<small>ONDAY, AND</small> I <small>WAS TWO YEARS, EIGHT MONTHS, AND</small> twelve days old. Dad stood next to me. His hair was longer and blonder then. I sat on the counter of my kitchen, right on top of the dishwasher.

Behind the dining table was one big window separated into three of equal size. The window almost reached the floor. Outside was our driveway, a field of cows, and a dozen 150-year-old maple trees. The sun was up, glinting off the melted snow. Spring was springing.

Beside me, as I sat above the dishwasher, a cooled hard-boiled egg was perched in a pink, plastic egg holder. I couldn't hold my egg because I was terrified I'd drop it. Although it was hard-boiled to specifically prevent egg-splatter mess, that didn't mean the shell wouldn't crack if the egg suddenly hit a hard surface. I didn't like the way the egg felt in my hand either.

Dad held his egg in his hand. He painted with yellow. I painted with pink. Then we painted another one for Mom together, using blue, because that was her favorite color. I wondered what color the new baby would choose.

Dad guessed, "Orange!"

Mom was in the hospital preparing for her C-section. She had Graham the next day, after Easter, and didn't come home for a few days.

I didn't know how babies were made, or even where they came from or how one would get into my house. Then Graham appeared in our three-bedroom country home, with orange hair and a gross belly button. I previously occupied the bedroom next to my parents', but I moved to the spare at the opposite end of the hall so the baby could be closer to our parents. I was not happy about the change. My parents bought me new bedding—"new, big girl stuff"—and tried to explain that the baby was going to need their attention more and needed to be close. I understood that, even though it made me upset.

The first time I saw him, he was laid out over a blanket on our old, dark-brown couch. It was so worn that it was really soft. It was deep, and part of a set of three, which included a love seat and my favorite chair.

A light shone on Graham's fragile little body as part of his jaundice treatment. I couldn't take my eyes off him. I knew he was going to be my best friend for the rest of my life. I loved him. I wanted to protect him. At the same time, I was scared to be around him, scared I was going to hurt him somehow.

Graham looked different from the rest of us, which made him more special. My father is blond, as am I, and my mom has dark brown hair. Graham's strange orangey-red hair influenced a name change. He was born during the SARS (severe acute respiratory syndrome) outbreak in 2003, and so he had to be a scheduled C-section (I've joked with my mom that he was not birthed but instead removed like a tumor). Before his removal, my family intended to call him Jack or Jax. My father's name is John, and his father's name is John, and his father's name was John. My mom was not about to name my brother John, but she'd settle for a derivative. When my brother was born with his orangutan-looking head, my parents looked at each other and they both knew that he was supposed to be a Graham. I don't know why red hair = Graham, but it does. If I found out one day that my name was supposed to be one thing and then was changed, I would find that really hard. Graham never seemed to mind.

As the days went by, our living room flooded with friends of my parents, all eager to gawk at their newest and proudest achievement. It was clear to me that my brother was born popular. Someone picked me up to see over the adults' heads. I spoke, but no one paid attention. Looking down at the busy, happy room, I realized everyone was looking at this baby and not at me. Sure, Graham was really cool, but so was I—yesterday. I wasn't mad at him (no one could be mad at Graham), but I was confused, and maybe a little jealous.

I worried I was going to have more needs and troubles than him. I'd already been on this Earth for two years and eight months and fifteen days; therefore, I was supposed to know more and be able to help. Graham needed more than I did physically because he had a smaller, newer, more fragile body. But emotionally, he already seemed to be a relaxed baby, rarely crying. He gave the instant impression that he was going to be easygoing. Out the gate, Graham proved to be spontaneous and flexible. This made me happy as much as it reminded me how different I was. I was never easygoing, even at two years old. I was scared that my seemingly happy-go-lucky, bouncy little redheaded brother was going to be so chill that he'd get frustrated with me. I worried we wouldn't get along and he wouldn't understand me.

When he was a newborn, I didn't have anything in common with him. I didn't need my diaper changed, I didn't spit up all over myself, and I could not only roll over and sit up and crawl, but I could also walk and run and skip pretty well. If I was away from my parents, I could probably survive more than two hours. I didn't enjoy Graham's loud and flashy baby toys. He didn't know many words, so he couldn't sing the songs I loved, my favorite being "Teddy Bears' Picnic." He didn't like to wear dresses. He actually enjoyed bath time. The one thing we had in common was that we both knew we loved each other, and we both knew that the other one loved us back just as much. We never needed confirmation; we never needed reassurance. We had an instant bond that never gave way.

He cried less and less as he grew up. He was a very content kid. He loved cars and had dozens of miniatures set up on the floor of his room, with a carpet that had a road-map pattern. He had ramps and funky machines that he put the cars in to make them do all kinds of tricks. Graham also loved tractors, so much so that my grandfather, who we called Papa, took him for rides on his backhoe. This was such a frequent occurrence that my brother's first word was "beep," mimicking the sound the backhoe made when it was backing up.

Unlike Graham, when I was tiny, I was a colicky baby. I cried a lot and was upset often. This didn't stop. Not when I was two. My parents, juggling me and a new baby, turned away from my screaming fits. Everything felt wrong all of the time, and I didn't even know why but I couldn't stop screaming. I needed help. I screamed more. I cried more than Graham, even though he was younger, which made me feel guilty. I felt like I needed my parents' time and attention, and they didn't have it to give. Eventually, I learned that my huge emotions made my parents turn away from me. They didn't know what to do, and so they pulled back.

"Paige, you're not going to get what you want just because you cry," they told me. "We know what you're trying to do and it's not working."

Yet still I had meltdowns and temper tantrums. I didn't mean to. But the feelings inside were overwhelming. I needed help. And no one knew how to help me.

> *i cannot control my thoughts*
> *i cannot control my feelings*
> *i simply*
> > *observe*
> > > *and listen*

Sometimes my parents read me a book before bed, primarily fables, Disney stories, tales about princesses and princes and animals and happy endings. I only enjoyed a few familiar stories and demanded they be constantly repeated, despite my parents' protests to try something new. From this committed repetition (an autism thing) came script memorization (I'm sure all kids do this as they learn to read, but it came so easily to me, which is also an autism thing we'll get to later).

My father knew I memorized the stories and tried to test me. As he read a story to me, he started to go off book, making up his own story with his own thoughts and ideas. I never let him get away with it. I wanted my story. I knew he wasn't telling my story right, and I had to correct him, because it was important to me that information was correct. I knew he was making up words. And I got so good at this detection that I could tell if he skipped a simple word, like "the" or "was" or "and." I'd memorized every single one. As time went by, I took that memorization and used it when my parents had to be with my brother.

I went into my room at the end of the hall, took out my books, and "read" them. I didn't know how to read or what words meant or what they looked like, but I did know the story audibly. I would then repeat the story and try to match it up with the words I saw on the page.

I saw the moments when my parents flipped the page. I knew after which phrases they pointed to the pictures in the book. I used these landmarks to help guide me along my path of reading. The books my parents read to me when I was little could be long and challenging. Any reading at all is challenging for a two-year-old, let alone reading at the level my parents did. But I did it.

Once I knew a few stories, I started finding patterns between them. That helped teach me how certain words were spelled. Once I learned how to spell individual words and could associate them with their meaning and their sound, I started to read other stories.

Anytime I didn't know how to say a word, I would burst out of my bedroom and run up to my parents and say, "Can you please tell me what this says?"

"Sound it out," my dad said.

"What does this word say?"

"Maybe we can read together later," Mom replied.

"What does this word mean?" I begged.

"We're busy right now, babe."

I never liked not knowing. I wish that I had access to Google when I was young, because I truly treated my parents like a search engine.

Children are constantly and consistently asking *why* when they're around two or three. *Why do these things happen? Why does this exist in this way? Why does it do that?* I was brand new at existing and had no idea what anything was. I wanted to know. Not only was I new to this world, but my books showed me more worlds. It was all so much information and not enough at the same time.

Once I started the *why* questions, I never stopped.

My parents were annoyed, I thought, because I was talking too much. I later found that the real reason was because I asked so many questions that they didn't know the answers to. We were all frustrated when they didn't have the answers.

As I got older, I wrote down my questions and tried to calculate reasonable answers.

> Why is the sky blue? It must have something to do with the sun, because the sky is not blue when there is no sun. Maybe if I know what the sun is, I can figure it out. I don't have a book about the sun, but I do have one about the solar system. Perhaps I will find sun answers in there, and then maybe I will have sky answers.

I was so helpless and young and stressed. I felt like the world was out of control, that it was unacceptable for me not to know the answers. So, whatever I came up with, I chose to believe. And there was one person who trusted me completely and would help me believe in my answers: Graham.

He didn't know any better. He wasn't smarter or older or more knowledgeable, and I definitely used that to my advantage. My goal wasn't to convince him I was right. I wanted to share the answers I came up with in the form of stories. He enjoyed the stories, and I relaxed by convincing myself that everything I said was correct. So, Graham was the recipient of all of my questionable question endeavors.

I searched for answers, not just for me but for him someday. I was determined to be equipped for when he began asking the *why* questions, so I could help him understand the world. Then he could have all of the answers and wouldn't be stressed. It was becoming more and more obvious that he was different from me: calmer, more relaxed, more easygoing, more loveable. But still, I had to learn everything so Graham could learn everything too.

If he asked why the sky was blue one day, I wanted to be able to tell him that it had more to do with the air, not just the sun.

My brother never complained when I crept into his crib and recited my stories to him. He didn't complain when I made him sit in a chair while I stood in front of him with a little chalkboard and tried to teach him. He didn't complain when I tried to get him to say the words I pointed to in a book, so that he could learn to read too.

The more time I spent doing something with my brother, the less time either of my parents needed to take care of us. They were enthused about the positive time we spent together.

"You're our little storytelling genius," Mom said.

So, Graham and I started reading. There were times as Graham got older when he did not wish to spend his free time being read to by his older sister, so he took out his little toy cars or his monster trucks or his tractors and started playing, while I continued to read aloud. Graham always listened, even if he didn't necessarily want to. He did because he wanted me to be happy. He always wanted me to be happy. Graham never made a decision that he thought would hurt me or make me upset. Graham is my closest family member, and that continues to this day. We were so different from each other, and kept being different, but it was okay. We understood each other, even though we had different brains. I always felt safe when Graham was around. I still do.

Graham never told me to stop crying, but sometimes he cried because I cried. It upset him. That upset me. It felt like he looked up to me, respected me, and I felt like his big sister in the world. I wanted to stop crying all the time for him. And for me. And for my parents.

But I couldn't.

I didn't know how.

My parents didn't know how to help me either. They got frustrated; they walked away; they often ignored me, hoping that would help. They seemed to think that I wanted attention, and that it would make things worse for me if they gave me that attention. This led to me feeling that I was being manipulative.

I felt more and more like I was wrong somehow. Being me was lonely and confusing. And those feelings only got worse as I entered the bigger world. Suddenly, it wasn't the world of my storybooks, a world I could control with my little brother by my side. A world that I could memorize.

I was about to start junior kindergarten, age four. And the world was going to get a whole lot more confusing.

CHAPTER 3

I MISS MOMMY AND DADDY

literally

"looking back there were signs that i never
realized to take things seriously

when i said to you
. . . i say this often . . .
'hold on, hold on to your shorts'
you would literally
hold on to your
shorts"

~ my mom

STOOD AT THE END OF OUR DRIVEWAY WITH MY PARENTS AND Graham. My mom's hand was squeezing mine tighter than my father's as the four of us waited. The cows were still out in the field, so the crisp autumn air mostly smelled like manure. My hair was in two pigtails on top of my head, the kind that just have the top layer, so it was still down but pulled back from my face.

I was crying. Mom was crying. Even Graham was crying. Everyone was nervous, especially me.

I'd seen the school bus drive by before, but I'd never been this close. It was a huge, loud, scary monster. I had never heard a vehicle sound that way before. Although it was scary, I felt a sort of empathy. The bus didn't ask to be big and scary. It probably didn't want to be that loud. The bus didn't mean to frighten me. It was a monster, but it was a monster that was supposed to keep me safe and wanted me to come along. It was a good monster.

We walked around the long, yellow stick flung out in front of the bus to get to the door on the other side. At the bottom of the stairs in front of an open door, Ron the driver greeted me. His voice made me feel safe, because it was the exact same voice that had called our house phone a week prior to introduce himself.

I was right where I was supposed to be.

I let go of my parents' hands, grabbed the railing, and pulled myself up the deep stairs with my right foot first, sobbing as I left my family. I looked back at them and then made my way, still crying.

One, two, three, four stairs onto the bus.

Ron looked like Santa Claus. I was never scared of him. He was not a man who commanded fear; I respected him. But, that first day, he was a stranger and I had to trust him to take me to a place I did not know. That did not mean I saw him as anything positive. Trusting this old, strange man in a yellow monster machine to take me to a new place away from my family, away from my food, away from my toys, away from my routine, and away from my life was not my definition of safety.

He said, "Come on in, Paige," and told me to take a seat.

This was the first time I ever had to take a seat.

Of course, I'd sat down thousands of times, in a bunch of places. At my kitchen table, I had sat at the head facing the kitchen window. But my parents eventually moved me to the opposite end of the table, with my back to the window, because at night, when it was dark outside, I would just stare at myself in the reflection rather than eat. I did not enjoy having my back to the window because that made me feel unsafe. I constantly turned around to look because I felt exposed. Shortly thereafter, I had a new position at the kitchen table, and that position was to the right of my mom, across from my father, with my brother beside Dad, across from Mom. When I took a seat at the kitchen table, I knew where I was sitting.

I had a seat in the living room as well, my chair that was my own. My chair:

- It was never meant to be my chair, but I'd adopted it.
- It was brown, deep, and soft, like the couches, and located in the perfect spot in the room, in front of the window.
- This window faced the same way as the one in the kitchen, but it was much larger. The sunrise and the sunset happened visibly from my chair—both, because the window is so wide, and the chair was placed just right.
- With the main overhead light and lamps, I could see well when I was reading in my chair.
- It was at a perfect angle to watch the TV.
- It was located in the best space in the living room, temperature-wise.
- It was clawed up on one side from my cat, Kitty. She also appreciated lying in the sun in my chair. And I liked sitting with her in that chair.

When my parents moved things around, they always kept the chair in the same place. If they didn't, I'd get upset. I'd try to live with it, but it was always worse, and I wanted it to go back to normal. My parents always put it back in the perfect spot.

I knew where I was going to sit in the living room.

The bus had way too many rows, the most options for seating I had ever seen. The door shut behind me. I didn't have a lot of time before the bus would begin its transit to the next stop to pick up the next child.

I was frozen, but only for a brief moment, because I wasn't allowed to remain frozen for long. Otherwise my whole body would be flung to the back of the bus as it started moving again. I made a snap decision, and that was to take the very first seat I could see, directly behind Ron.

As I sat down, my tears streamed. The confusion, the frustration, the questions.

Did I pick the right seat? Was this my seat? Would I sit here again coming home? The next day? Did I steal someone else's seat by accident? Would I get kicked out of this seat? Was this a bad seat to choose? Would people think differently about me because of my seat choice? Should I have picked the seat opposite so that I could not see Mom crying as we left? I couldn't see the road now that I was seated directly behind the driver. Was that going to be okay? Why didn't anyone tell me where to sit? Why did I have to choose when I did not know all of the facts to make the correct choice? Should I change to the right side? No, I couldn't, because the bus was in motion.

I was crying but making no noise, just streams of tears and sobs I tried to swallow. Seeing my mom cry out the window as we departed made my tears come harder.

We went on a forty-five-minute journey to pick up other students before getting to school. About fifteen minutes into our route, we picked up a gaggle of students all at one stop. A girl climbed up onto the bus. She was at least three years older than me, a foot taller, and she wore a pink, zip-up sweater-vest with a hood and a light-blue skirt. Her outfit did not go together. She had two barrettes in her hair and wore a backpack.

I didn't notice until I heard Ron, the driver, say, "Keep going, Emily."

"I can't," she said. "Someone's sitting in my seat." She blocked the whole line of kids behind her.

I looked up to see her freckled face glaring down at me. Without words, I quickly got up and made a new seat choice, the quickest and most effective I could. I sat right behind her, two seats behind Ron.

I cried harder.

Later, Ron wrote our names on pieces of tape above our seats, so everyone knew where they were sitting and there'd be no seat taking.

No one asked me to move again. That seat became Paige's seat. I remained sitting in that exact seat every day, twice a day, for forty-five minutes to and from school, for the next eight years.

That first day, I cried for the entire journey. My eyes were red and sore. I couldn't speak, and my throat was raw and exhausted. I was full of snot but trying to look okay and be okay.

We arrived at my new school and it was time to get off the bus. As I was in the second row, I was one of the first to depart. Ron wished me a good day.

I didn't reply. I walked down the four stairs of the bus, with my right foot first, and suddenly I was on the concrete in front of the school. It was windy and gray out, and my sweater didn't warm me.

I stood there. Some kids went left, some went right, some went straight. I didn't know what to do, where to go, and everyone was so much taller than me.

It was the end of the world.

I started following the girl who had glared at me on the bus, *Emily*. She went left. As I followed, I thought: *Why was I trusting Emily? I didn't even think she really liked me that much. I stole her seat earlier. Did Emily know I was following her? Was she leading me into a trap? She seemed older. Were we even supposed to go to the same place?*

I turned around and started back toward the bus. Emily had turned left, so maybe I was supposed to turn right. Or perhaps I would just enter the school and try to find an adult who knew the layout and maybe my name.

The bus was gone. All I could see in front of me was a road with cars and people and no one paying any attention. I was powerless and scared. More tears.

I turned around again. If Emily was walking one way, it probably meant children could walk that way. Perhaps if I were to walk that way as well, even if I ended up in the wrong place, I would get to a place. A place was better than no place. But then I stopped again, staring at the children passing me. *What if the place I went to was the wrong place? And then what if no one knew where I was? And then they'd end up calling my mom, and she would get scared, and I'd be reported missing. Why didn't anyone tell me where to go? Why didn't my mom know where I was supposed to go, and tell me? What was the right answer?*

I stood there, crying more audibly and panicking. Breathing heavily. My vision was blurry, and my brain was numb, and I swore I was going to die right there . . . until I heard a friendly woman's voice.

"Are you lost?"

I wanted to be strong and powerful and in control at all times, and no one was allowed to know otherwise. But I turned to her.

Holding onto her hand was a little girl, and this little girl looked like me. She had blonde hair and blue eyes just like mine, except her blonde hair was lighter. It's very easy to tell with blue eyes if someone has been crying, because the red-and-blue contrast is impossible to miss. Like me, the other little girl had clearly been crying. She looked like she was holding the woman's hand, rather than the woman holding hers. I felt that if she could trust this woman, then perhaps I could as well.

The woman encouraged me to come with them, as she assumed I was headed to junior kindergarten, like the little girl. I didn't take her hand nor did I take the little girl's hand. I do not like to hold people's hands unless I have to.

I followed them with a numb brain and eventually got to the right classroom.

There was a designated cubby with my name on it to hang up my backpack and leave my belongings, so I went to that cubby and took my indoor shoes out of my bag and put them on. My shoes were Velcro, but some kids had laces on their shoes already, and that made me feel behind. The little blonde girl put her shoes on too. She came up to me when she was done and asked me if I wanted to sit next to her on the carpet. Her name was Molly. She was my best friend and my only friend for the whole first year of junior kindergarten.

I had a spot when Molly was there.

Some kids' parents dropped them off right at the classroom door, which meant I witnessed a good amount of crying on the first day. The other kids crying meant that I didn't stand out anymore and no one looked at me. I was doing what I was supposed to. I was having an appropriate first-day reaction.

Crying was even an appropriate second-day reaction. By the third day, there was a lot less crying, but everyone understood if you did. I saw lots of children cry as they left their parents the first week. I heard people call out for their mom when they got hurt on the play-ground, or say they needed their mom when they felt sick and had to go home.

By the end of the first week, most of the crying had ceased altogether.

I cried every single day of junior kindergarten. I cried while we were on the carpet reading. I cried during nap time. I cried at lunch. I cried when I played in the sandbox and while changing my indoor and outdoor shoes. Sometimes my crying got so intense that I asked to go to the single-stall bathroom at the back of the class so I could shut the door and be alone and cry as loudly as I needed.

I hated going to school. It was so loud and so much. The lights buzzed. Everyone talked over each other all the time. I'd never been in a building with so many people talking. People bumped into me and touched me. I didn't like how dirty everything was. I didn't like sharing. I didn't ever know what to do.

But I didn't mean to cry. I don't even remember thinking of something that then made me cry. It felt uncontrollable and unrea-sonable and never-ending. I tried to hide my tears as much as I could and not have everyone stare at me and interrupt the teacher.

"You're okay, Paige. Everything is okay," Mrs. Reynolds said when I was crying. She held puppets. She smiled. "Come on, Paige," she pleaded. "All the other kids are missing their mommies and daddies, but they're not crying."

The other kids asked me what was wrong when they saw me cry. They noticed my unhappiness and wanted to make it better. But I couldn't begin to describe what was wrong. Sometimes, I'd be hold-ing myself together as best I could, only for the smallest inconve-nience to send me down a wailing spiral.

- I put my shoes on the wrong feet and had to redo them.
- I got sand in my eyes.

- My raspberries tasted funny.
- Someone didn't put the cap on my favorite marker properly so it dried up.
- Someone tried to kiss me.
- I couldn't hold scissors correctly.
- I hated the puppet my teacher used to read us a story.

None of these were the *real* reasons for my tears; they were final triggers. But I never knew why I felt so dysregulated all the time. Molly put her head on my shoulder, and said, "It's okay. You have me. I'm your best friend." Even though I was crying, this made me feel safe. Comforted.

"Why are you crying, Paige?" she asked.

Eventually, I said, "I miss Mommy and Daddy."

There were a lot of things that were hard to deal with: transitions, the kids, the mess, loud sounds, the smells, my lack of autonomy, interacting with kids who were mean, that everyone was a stranger and bigger than me and terrifying. But that's not what I said, because that's not something I knew, yet.

Graham stayed home while I went to junior kindergarten, senior kindergarten, and grade one, because he was still too small for school. My parents worked during the day, so Graham was often watched by grandparents or family friends. I liked when it was our grandparents because then he stayed home, and I got to see him right when I got off the bus. Graham and Grandma stood at the end of the driveway to collect me after school and walk me back down the driveway to our house. Graham waddled over, smiling ear to ear, and for the next twenty minutes I got a recap of their adventures that day.

Grandma took my backpack and began emptying it on the counter, while Graham and I ran into his room, took out a set of farm toys that we shared, and played with them, probably for hours.

Mom came home, and we manipulated animal figurines on the bedroom floor.

I was terrified that one day I would come home to find the head off one of the cows or dents in the sheep, because Graham was not as gentle with his toys as I was with mine. So I asked him to make sure not to play with our farm animals if I wasn't there.

"I won't," he said.

I just wanted to prevent how crushed I'd be if he broke my toy.

Sharing anything was a very big deal and incredibly difficult for me. Sharing with a destructive baby? Who I loved so much? Oh my god. The willpower. The strength. The horror. The fire I felt constantly in my chest when he banged the horse's leg on the floor. But I loved him and I couldn't be mean to him, even though I felt like exploding. So, sometimes I took the toy away. I needed to do *something* to control my environment—to control him—to make the burning stop. I tried to be fair. I tried to explain. I tried to say, "You're not playing nice with a toy we share. I'm scared you're going to break it, and that makes me very upset. Please play with one of your own toys and I'll let you use this again when you are ready to treat it with respect."

"Paige!" he cried. "Mom!" he cried next.

There were only a handful of moments when Graham really got upset. We solved problems ourselves most of the time, but there was once when Mom got involved.

"Paige . . . give your brother his toy back." She sounded disinterested, appeasing Graham for Graham's sake.

"No, Mom. I can't. Not until he's nice with my toys." I couldn't hold back sobs.

Graham was crying, and he rarely cried. I really didn't like that. I didn't know he was going to be so upset. I brought the toy out and tried to show the marks on the horse's leg inflicted by Graham, at which time Mom and Graham stopped caring. Graham did something else, and Mom did something else.

I put the horse back in Graham's room and ran into mine and shut the door and cried for doing that to my brother.

I could never do anything right, and I never made anything better.

Junior kindergarten was every other day. I had one day of normal life: a routine I was familiar with, with my room and my books and my brother and no shoes and no noise and no kids. The next day, I was torn away from all that to be around loud kids who did loud things. I had to sit crisscross applesauce on the prickly carpet. It was a thin mat and the fabric was sharp. I had to listen to a boring story while the lights screamed at me, and the events and routines changed every day and couldn't be anticipated. Then back to safety at home the next day.

On the days when I had school, I had a crying fit afterward that I took into my room, for hours. Alone. My blue walls welcomed me with a hug every time I entered. I never felt like a stranger there, whereas at school, the white brick walls were cold and empty.

I had a three-piece bedroom set: a bed frame, a bedside table, and a dresser. Everything was white, and the edges were trimmed with crown molding. Pretty and girly. The knobs on all of the drawers were white with a picture stamp of a bouquet of flowers. The flowers were pink and yellow and periwinkle.

On top of my dresser, a large mirror was attached, littered with stickers I'd collected over the years. My cluttered dresser held a collection of lip glosses, hair accessories for me and my dolls, a large radio accompanied by a larger stack of CDs, books, and clean clothes I hadn't put away. I had an alarm clock on my nightstand with Cinderella on it, and when a button was pressed, the background of Cinderella's landscape lit up in a dim purple light, highlighting the princess's silhouette. It was my night-light and my alarm clock.

When I used that alarm clock, I kept the alarm set for 7:15 a.m. I always woke up before my alarm on school days. I tried to fall asleep before 9:11 p.m. I knew 911 was not a good sequence of numbers, so I thought that the time also wasn't lucky. If I knew I was still awake at that time, it would be bad, so I kept my eyes closed in bed and refused to look at the clock.

My twin bed had a canopy that made me feel protected. The trim on the canopy was laced with yellow and blue ribbons and embroidered with bows, lace, and beads in the shapes of flowers. Curtains hung down from all four pillars of the canopy, closing at night around the bed. A princess throw blanket was draped over the floral comforter, toward the side. The princesses on the blanket faced me as I climbed in.

My mom insisted that canopy beds were kept in the middle of their bedroom due to all of the fabric; I insisted on keeping my bed in the corner of the room, farthest away from the door and closest to the window. I felt like there was more space in my bedroom that way. And I could have my back to the wall and not to an empty space, leaving me vulnerable to ghosts and other nightly predators.

I went into this familiar space at the end of a school day, and I screamed and collapsed. I cried and yelled, and this would go on for hours.

"Paige, stop crying. Everyone goes to school," Mom said. "What happened? What's so bad?"

I was sobbing so hard, I couldn't speak. And even if I could, I had nothing to say. Nothing was so bad, yet everything was.

"In our house, we go to school unless we're broken or bleeding," Mom said. "You'll go again next time. It's fine. Everything's fine."

And then, when I still wouldn't stop sobbing: "There's nothing wrong, Paige," Mom said. "You being upset and stressed is normal. Everyone feels this way about school. Just stop crying. It's *fine*."

My brain didn't understand what she meant. If everyone else felt this way, then why weren't they this upset? Were other kids crying at home like this? None of them seemed upset at school.

Molly wasn't upset. We spent recess together. I sat with her on the carpet. Everything was easier when she did it with me. All I wanted to do was whatever she was doing. I sat beside Molly during lunch, but if Molly wasn't there, things would get more difficult. I sat by myself, away from anyone who had already formed a group. My spot was beside Molly. Where was it if she wasn't there?

At the end of junior kindergarten, Molly left my school. I was devastated and felt like I'd never find another friend like that again. At that stage of my life, kids were friendly and tried to connect, but they weren't like Molly. I missed her. I didn't know how to navigate school without her, but I had to, whether I was ready or not.

CHAPTER 4

THE BACK RIGHT CORNER OF THE CLASS

anywhere

when can i just exist and have that
be enough?

~ twenty-year-old me

I WASN'T INTERESTED IN THE SAME THINGS AS THE OTHER KIDS. I didn't like being loud or crashing toys or mixing the Play-Doh and making a mess or being sticky or running into other kids or falling on the ground and getting grass stains on my knees. But I did enjoy books.

In first grade, to begin our reading journey, we had books labeled alphabetically by difficulty. The easiest level was AAA. Then came AA, then A, and then B, C, D, all the way up to Z. It was expected that, to begin, as we were different people, we would all be somewhere in the A gradient, working up to a Z reading level by grade six.

We checked out three or four books at our level per week when our class had library time. It was then our job to read all the books within a week. We read aloud with an adult at home, who marked a sheet to record our progress. Each week, my teacher Mrs. Hendry looked over the sheets to influence the curriculum based upon sounds or words we were having trouble with, and also to decide when to increase the reading level.

AAA was the basic level, with only one sentence per page.

- "I like cats," with a picture of a cat.
- "I like dogs," with a picture of a dog.
- "I like cows," with a picture of a cow.

I flipped through fast and stopped paying attention. I went on to an AA book. It wasn't much more difficult. I increased to level A and brought four home. Mom and I sat on my perfect chair in the living room and read through all those books in only a few minutes. Mom marked on the sheet that I was bored and not being challenged, so Mrs. Hendry moved me up to a B reading level. Mom noted the same thing. I was then promoted to level C. Mom wrote that I needed more.

I'd read *Heidi* by Johanna Spyri, a four-hundred-page book for preteens, before I was four, before I started junior kindergarten. I read *Are You There God? It's Me, Margaret* and the Nancy Drew mystery *The Secret of the Old Clock* next. At the time, I was young, so I didn't know how other kids' brains formed patterns of words. Years later, I discovered how unusual my reading was. In grade eleven, I helped teach grade one kids reading by taking them one by one into the hall. I really loved teaching kids. I liked how they approached the world so very much as themselves, unafraid to ask questions. Grade eleven Paige enjoyed whipping out those little AAA, AA, and A booklets to read aloud with small children. There was a list of over a hundred sight words, and the goal was to have the students read all of the sight words by the end of the year. I worked with every single one of the kids in that class. The experience shook me to my core because I realized how different I'd been, and how obvious it was.

They read like six-year-olds. They needed to learn how to read "out," "about," "down." They don't see or hear the patterns in those words and instantly get it, like I do.

Mrs. Hendry's desk was in the back corner of the room. There was a discolored patch on the ceiling above, like something had smashed through it and it had to be repaired in a DIY fashion.

"That hole is there because, one year, my class just drove me so nuts that I was sitting at my desk and I got so angry that my head spun right off and went right through the roof!" she said.

"You can't do that!" The class laughed and giggled. "No, you're lying right now to us!"

But she persisted. She crossed her arms with a grin. "Oh, I'm serious. And if you guys drive me crazy enough, one day, you'll see it too!"

There were times when I thought her head was going to spin off and soar through the roof, but thankfully we weren't bad enough to make that happen.

Mrs. Hendry sat me down at her desk, facing her directly. We spoke quietly because the class was silent reading. She had gray hair and a happy face I loved talking to.

"So, Paige. How's reading going?" she said.

"It's okay," I replied. "It's just really boring."

"Yeah?"

I nodded, smiling so she didn't think I was angry.

"I read what your mom wrote down here in your notes. She said you guys flew through these books pretty fast too, huh?"

"Yeah, we did."

"Your mom said these books were still too easy for you. Did you think they are too easy?"

"I don't know," I said. "I don't know what harder looks like."

"Can we try reading this book together?" She pulled out a book from my reading bag that I'd already read at home. It was called *The Final Race*. She reached across the desk to place it in front of me.

"Do you want me to read it?" I asked. I didn't know how to read something "together." Did she want us both to say the words aloud at the same time? Did she want to point with her finger and have me follow along? Were we going to share holding the book?

"Yes, please," she replied.

Okay. I opened the book on top of her desk, so she could see and tell me if I read any words wrong.

"I run fast in a race with my friends alongside the field where the tall grass grows . . ."

"Okay." She turned around and sifted behind her desk through bins of books. She pulled out books from various levels. One by one, we read the first few pages of these books "together," which meant I read them out loud and she did absolutely nothing but listen.

I fumbled on a word here or there as we reached the last few levels: Y and Z. Words I'd never seen before like "sophisticated" or "advantageous." I sounded them out.

"Hmm. Looks like you're all done." She shrugged her shoulders and lifted her palms up to her ears. "It seems like you've read everything you need to read. You pass grade one!" She grinned at me.

"Wow, okay," I said. "Uh . . . does this mean I have nothing to read anymore?" I hoped to be done with *those* books, as they were really boring in general. I wasn't interested in them. But I still wanted to read. I wanted to get new books every week like everyone else.

"No, you're still gonna read," she said. "Do you think anyone's gonna make you stop reading?" She was joking—that was a joke. We shared a laugh, genuinely.

"You're going to read more of what you want," she continued. "You'll still get new books every week, but instead, you'll get more of a choice. I don't have the books for you in the classroom, but I bet they do in the library."

"They do!" I got very excited. The library was full of books I wished to read. Books about sharks and ghosts and bugs and the moon and origami and knitting. So that's what we did. The librarian had a list of books just for me, as comparable to the curriculum, and I chose one of those books each week.

Mrs. Hendry still called me over to her desk when it was my turn on the roster during silent reading time, and I read to her to confirm I was still on track.

I really liked having the freedom to read a bit more of what I wanted, and the trust that the teacher had in me. I felt independent. I didn't need help from my parents or my teacher. So, they left me to my own devices.

My reading journey continued in the library. I was allowed to go and pick out books. The teachers thought it best if I still read fiction, as those novels designed for young readers often contained similar language to that of the curriculum. Nonfiction books—where I could learn all of the species of birds and their Latin names, or every muscle in the body, or types of clouds and how precipitation worked—had very different vocabulary. Even though I found those books more interesting, I had to keep them for entertainment only.

I really enjoyed Mrs. Hendry as my teacher. She made learning fun and the classroom seem okay. Drama was my favorite class ever, and Mrs. Hendry was the first teacher who introduced it to me. She did a period of drama with us every Friday, where we played funny acting games with props and silly costumes.

Once Mom found out I liked drama class, she found a local kids' theater company and signed me up for my first out-of-school play. It was the first kind of after-school activity that I really liked and continued. I quit everything else I tried, with a lot of tears along the way: swimming, horseback riding, soccer, dance (which I returned to, in seven years). The first time I went to theater, I packed an over-the-shoulder bag filled with some of my favorite things to comfort me: a butterfly journal and pink feather pen, a mini snow globe from Jamaica, a Ziploc baggie of Goldfish crackers, an eraser from school that smelled good, two pencils, a pink highlighter, mittens in case it got cold, indoor slippers, and a hair elastic, just in case. The director gave me a script and asked me to read it out loud. I liked reading out loud, and I did it quickly and accurately.

I was happy in theater, and I was good at it. I was a good actor and I was easy to work with because I followed directions very well. I had found something that was safe and real and mine.

My permanent desk location became the back right corner of the class. I was content because my seat didn't change every month along with the rest of the class, and no one sat beside me who could bother me or talk to me or touch my pencils or pretty erasers. It was even better when everyone was called to the carpet, because then they were even farther away. As I was ahead with reading, and carpet time was reading time, I was allowed to stay at my desk, alone. I liked being alone. And I liked how everyone faced away from me, not looking at me.

My name tag was taped onto the desktop, along the left side. The teacher wrote our names for us, but we got to decorate the background on our first day of school. Mine just had a bunch of hearts on it, because I didn't know what else to draw. That was fine. I liked how it looked. I used a lot of purple and pink.

Alone at this desk of mine, the loud, stressed-out part of my brain went away. School was about doing things, and I did the best things when I was alone. I could just do the tasks I was assigned. I didn't have to be anything. I didn't have to slow down and do things like the other kids.

I had worksheets and textbooks and activities to keep myself occupied. Some days, a high school teacher came to instruct me. While the other kids learned about the sounds different vowels made, I learned about the invention of the telephone. While they wrote sentences, I wrote essays. While they were read to, I scoured encyclopedias and took notes about subjects I found interesting and topics I wanted to learn more about. I was focused on school and learning. It was fun. I had a nickname from one kid. He called me "Busy Bee, because you're always busy! Work, work, work, your head in a book." I was six. That school year had a lot of learning and joy for me, even though the noise and the chaos were still hard. And I was excited that Graham started junior kindergarten when I started grade two.

Graham went to the same junior kindergarten class that I went to on my first day. It was perfect! I knew exactly where to go, and I told him plenty of times so he wouldn't forget, and I figured I could walk him to class.

Once we got off the bus, the teachers waiting there told us to hurry inside, because our bus ran a little late and school was about to start. They wanted us to enter through the front doors, rather than walk around the school.

Now I had no idea what to do. Graham started crying. He looked around frantically, searching for anything familiar, and we locked eyes.

"Paigey!" he called as the line of kids he was in began to move. His little hands reached for me. His cry roared louder, as if to alert me to his whereabouts among the sea of small people.

But he needed to go into the school through that door, so his line kept going. I lost his eyes and then lost his whole person. Teachers ushered the herd of children through the open double doors. A tall row of neon vests blocked my way, and I couldn't get through.

"He doesn't know where to go!" I cried. I ran around the school to access the doors I was supposed to enter, and I raced into my classroom to alert my grade two teacher. "Hi. My name is Pa-Paige.

I just wanted to let you know that I'm here but I'm going to be late. I have to g-g-go show my brother where his class is, and I'll be right back."

"Paige! Stay here, hun." The teacher began talking to other students and walked away from me.

I followed. "No. He's in junior kindergarten. He doesn't know where he's going. I'll be back." I needed her to know where I was, so I would be covered for attendance and no one would worry. *Hear me.*

She didn't.

"I'll be back!" I hurried down the hall away from my classroom, toward Graham's.

"Paige! Come back!" I heard my teacher call, but I pretended I was too far out of earshot to hear her. I continued my mission until I was stopped by an educational assistant who worked with some kids in my old class. We called her Ms. V.

Ms. V saw me walking toward the primary hall, crying, and stopped me. "Whoa, Paige, turn around. That's not where class is."

I ignored her.

"Paige!"

"No, Ms. V, I'm sorry." I was sobbing from the conflict I faced: that of breaking the rules but also needing to help Graham.

"Where are you going?" She was at my side now.

"My brother—" I kept walking. "Graham is lost."

"You don't have to worry about him. I'll make sure he's okay." She reached for my hand.

"No!" I yanked my hand away. "I need to know he's okay *right now.*"

"Okay! Okay. I'll go find him. Come on."

"Please call the office or call Mrs. Reynolds right now and make sure Graham got to class. Please, can you?" I begged Ms. V. "Graham. He's four and he has red hair."

Ms. V used a classroom phone to call down to Mrs. Reynolds's junior kindergarten room to check in on Graham. I stood right next to the phone with my ear up as high as it could go to listen to as much of the conversation as possible. It was a very short discussion.

"Mrs. Reynolds says that Graham made it there, all safe and sound. She said he's playing with some of the other kids and having fun."

Oh.

"Are you sure?" I asked. I felt like I was being lied to.

"Yep. So, are you good to change into your indoor shoes now and go to class?" said Ms. V.

Without saying anything, I walked away.

Crybaby

the panic on his little face in the crowd

    i couldn't imagine what happened between now and then

    what made him able to forget about that fear and happily play instead?

    i tried to force myself to stop crying before i got in the classroom.

    the last thing i needed was to make a crybaby impression again.

Graham didn't think I was different. The fact that I seemed sensitive and cried a lot was fine to him. He was always so happy, carefree, chill, and quiet. He was relaxed and barely spoke at all. I was the diva, the drama queen who took theater. I was also the sister who did well at school, whereas Graham struggled with academics. He was great at sports and he loved to play hockey. He also played soccer and lacrosse. Graham was also great at having friends, and he got invited to birthday parties all the time. Each time a kid in his grade had a birthday party, Graham was invited. I rarely was.

At home, Graham was always outside with Dad being loud and dirty, and I was inside, doing whatever Paige did. We were opposites. But having him at school that year was a comfort and a joy.

As soon as I began grade three, my teacher discontinued the program where I studied at my desk alone and had high school teachers come in to teach me. I didn't know it at the time, but she thought it was important I learned with the rest of my peers. She told my parents that it would be beneficial for me to fit in and be like everyone else. I never thought someone would purposely hold me back because they thought it was best for me. Fitting in wasn't a priority for me; I just wanted to feel good.

But then, once I was with the rest of my class, it became apparent that I wasn't like everyone else. I stood out everywhere. Learning with the other kids, I realized I learned very differently. And I couldn't understand why. I was just like everyone else—my mom told me so, my brother thought so, and apparently this teacher did too. I started judging myself. I compared myself to the other students and how they never had to work as hard to get through the day as I did. I cried every day at home after school.

On snowy days when the school buses were canceled, Dad was the one who usually took Graham and me to school, because Mom wasn't ready to go to work that early. Dad left for work at the same time that our bus picked us up.

He drove a Ford pickup truck with ladders and wood hanging out the back. Inside, the three of us sat on a bench-like seat, with me on the far right because I needed a window seat, and Graham needed the middle to be able to watch the speedometer go up and down.

Dad played our town's local radio station in the morning, to get news and weather and hit songs from back when he was a kid. "Jailhouse Rock" came on the radio as we rolled into town. Dad made an "oh" sound and reached for the volume knob. Graham and I looked at each other and giggled. Dad loved Elvis so much.

"What year did this song come out, Paigey?" Dad knew the answer. He was seeing if I did.

I didn't care about Elvis songs, but I cared about showing Dad I listened to him when he spoke about his passions. I made an educated guess. It sounded like older Elvis, which I assumed placed the song somewhere in the fifties. Later fifties, given his start . . .

"Fifty-seven?" I guessed.

"Yep!" He paused, coming up with another question for me. "This one will get ya. What year was Elvis's first gold record?" He looked over at me, smirking.

"Nineteen fifty-six." I smiled back at him because I knew I got it right.

"What song?"

"'Heartbreak Hotel.'" I answered. I knew that was right, too, because he'd asked me the same question two months ago.

"You're right. Name two other songs of his from that year."

I thought. "'Hound Dog'?"

"Yep, and?"

"I don't know . . . 'Blue Suede Shoes'?"

"Yep!" He was so excited I knew. "Both fifty-six. One of my favorite years."

Or he was excited about 1956. I hoped he saw that I cared.

Lunchtime was an exciting period for a lot of students in my class. I overheard them talking about what they thought would be in their lunch that day: soup or a sandwich or a bagel or hot dogs or pasta or leftovers. Sometimes they clapped when they found their lunch contained everything they were hoping for. Sometimes, they became upset or frustrated when their lunch didn't contain what they wanted. The kids traded snacks with each other.

I knew what was in my lunch every day and that I was going to like it, because it was always the same. Food has always been complicated for me. I had stomachaches often, and I don't know when I'm hungry. I can't feel that. I have to force myself to eat. I struggle with menus and food choices, and I'm often grossed out by food.

At lunchtime at school, I couldn't figure out why the other students didn't have the same meal every day like I did. It was clear they had preferences. I didn't grasp why a different daily lunch was necessary. The uncertainty would be stressful. *Why would anyone enjoy that uncertainty?* But the other kids seemed to like the up and down of not knowing; they found it thrilling and fun. The idea of opening my lunch box to find something new was anxiety provoking.

I knew what I was eating every time I opened my lunch box.

Bologna sandwich

- It was on white bread with mustard.
- The mustard was evenly spread along all corners of both pieces of bread.
- The sandwich was cut in half, separating the top and the bottom of the bread so the bottom half was a rectangle.
- The top half was from the top half of the loaf, so it had those top bumps.
- I ate the rectangle half first.
- I ate from the top left corner to the bottom right corner.
- Then, I grabbed the top half and did the same thing.
- I did this every day.

Sitting alone, I picked at my bologna sandwich. When I bit into a slab of bologna and tore away some meat, tiny little bits of bologna (because it's a weird, ground-up meat) almost poked out through my tooth-mark indentation from the previous bite. That looked like little hairs, like little eyebrow hairs, in my bologna. I knew, logically, they weren't hairs, but ever since I thought of that, I could not bite into that bologna until I was sure I had plucked all of the bologna hairs out. I took another bite of my sandwich and looked down to see bologna hairs.

Yep, again. Bologna hairs. You know what you have to do.

I sat and picked at my bologna in between white bread. Each "hair" I plucked, I tossed behind me.

I hope they vacuum here every day, otherwise, by the end of the year, there's going to be a pile of bologna hairs on the floor!

It became more and more apparent that the other kids knew something I didn't, something that made it okay to have a varied lunch. I was missing knowledge or skills that could help me deal with change better. I believed I was the same as everyone else, that they all felt the same way I did. Yet, I could see the evidence before my eyes that they had different priorities and notions of pleasure.

I studied humans more than I studied anything else, like they were a different species. Or I was.

FIELD NOTES

I wanted to learn their secrets and figure out what made them feel so prepared and in control that they could be simple and easygoing and relaxed.

It was like everyone had instructions, preprogrammed from birth, and I didn't have the manual. I was learning how to be human, but it seemed like the other kids had already figured it out.

It didn't seem like they were studying how to walk and talk and smile and introduce themselves.

They weren't studying how they liked their hair and how they spoke to authority figures and what to do when change happened or what to say when someone asked how they were.

I often thought of myself as an alien, like I was not a being of this planet or of this world or of this universe.

It felt like the other kids had been on Earth for so much longer than I had and they understood the rules, whereas I had to figure them out. All the time. All by myself.

The one thing I did know was that my ability to absorb, understand, and obtain information was something that this world considered really good. It was something that I didn't have to try to do, just my natural ability. Finally, something I could do well. Knowing that it was good, that I was getting praised, that people thought I was cool or good or doing something right because of this talent, made me think that I was going to be fine somehow.

I remember one girl came over to my quiet desk and asked, "How did you get perfect on this test? How did you know how to do that?"

"I just . . . repeat what I read," I replied.

And she smiled.

I began having friends in the class. Not a friend like Molly had been four years before, but people who were friendly with me and kind. I got invited to birthday parties. I was nice to people. Kids were nice to me. Some kids had similar hobbies to me now, like acting classes and reading books. I loved Littlest Pet Shops, tiny toys, and I collected lots, which other girls thought was cool.

The kids in class who I studied came to *me* with questions about math and science—questions I had the drive to figure out, the capacity to contain the answer to, and the ability to retrieve when necessary.

I didn't know

- How long I should look someone in the eye
- How to make showering bearable
- How to decide what to wear
- What my favorite color was
- How to cry at appropriate times
- How to eat all sorts of foods

I did know

- I was good with facts about anything other than being a person

Most of my classmates seemed to need help with facts. I could actually be useful. When they wanted information from me, they were nice and paid attention and said thank you. They would pick me to be their partner on school projects and we spent time together outside of school, as if we were friends. I lived with constant fear, discomfort, and stress that I wasn't right and I wasn't okay. I wanted to figure it out and understand what I didn't know: What was going on with me? I came to a conclusion: as long as I could know everything, I was going to be okay.

My conclusion was not correct.

CHAPTER 5

GRAPE JUICE BOX

special

what i own is mine
what i chose
graham and i both got the same candy at the grocery store
but mine was the one on the left and that was important
i didn't let the cashier mix them up or put them in the
same bag
that would make it impossible to differentiate
mine from his

WAS BORN AT 4:12 A.M. MY BROTHER WAS BORN SOMEWHERE around 10 a.m., my father was born around lunchtime, and my mom had no idea of her birth time. My father said he liked eating so much because he was born at lunchtime. Graham liked to sleep in and start his day slow because he was born at 10 a.m. And I couldn't sleep because I was born at night and wanted to start my day before everyone else.

FIELD NOTES

I think of my brain as female, like a boat or the Earth, doing her own thing in my skull. She feels separate from my body. My brain does so much that I don't get to control and that I don't want to happen.

My brain wasn't good at sleep.

Sleeping in made no sense to her.

Sleep was only a nuisance and punishment for inhabiting a human body.

She had things to do and think about.

To let me know she was done sleeping, she gave me dreams.

Scary dreams where I was stuck and unable to move. While being chased. Defenseless against something bad or where Graham was being hurt and I couldn't help.

Once I awoke, my brain got to business. She made my heart rate jump back up to where it liked to be during the day, which was almost double what it was at night. She got the ping-pong thoughts out and began to play table tennis with them.

Thoughts like: *My parents had spare time yesterday and didn't want to spend it with me. They really wanted to see less of me when they had spare time. Their spare time was for having their friends over, then being silly and drunk and swearing and talking about sex and ignoring me and hoping I'd go away. Graham didn't seem to mind, happily playing with cars or trucks and going to bed. Why doesn't any of this bother him like it bothers me?*

It was still dark outside, just after 4 a.m. and dead silent in the house.

My brain couldn't wait to get my hands on an art project every morning. I had numerous art kits. I made jewelry with beads and charms, or a model of a house out of paper and cardboard, or I tied pieces of fabric together to create a quilt. I didn't stay in bed longer than a minute. I had things to do.

This particular day was a Saturday and I was eight years old. My parents had friends over the previous night, and they'd been noisy as I was trying to sleep. They didn't go to bed until a few hours prior to my awakening because they were up drinking.

I did not like my parents very much when they had friends over. They didn't follow the rules they set for Graham and me, and their friends didn't follow the rules either. They made messes. They talked too loud indoors. They came in smelling of cigarettes. They wouldn't put a quarter in the swear jar every time they swore, and they called me annoying for pointing that out. This made me cry. But I think the worst part of all was that every time my parents had friends over, Mom and Dad ignored me.

The night before, I'd stayed in my room and cried. I buried my head in my pillows to drown out the sound of their obnoxious laughter and adult talk. I came out several times to tell them they needed to quiet down. One of the women responded back that Mommy and Daddy were trying to have a fun night and I was a bad kid for trying to stop them.

In the quiet dark of the house, I turned on the TV, and a game show for grown-ups came on. Hopefully, Mom would hear the babble of the guest contestants on the TV and know if she woke up, she could come out to hang out with me.

With the TV chatting away, I crossed the living room to get to the open-plan kitchen. The water cooler had a little fridge in the bottom and we stored juice boxes there, so I grabbed one myself without a chair. I drank a juice box every morning. This morning, there was only grape flavor left: my least favorite flavor. Grape was Graham's favorite. Not mine.

This grape-juice-box start meant my day was not going to be good.

I was probably being punished for being a bad kid the night before. It was my fault there were no fruit-punch juice boxes left.

All I deserved was a grape juice box.

It made me sad with myself. I was annoying the night before. I hadn't behaved like Graham did. I knew that my parents weren't going to be happy with me.

I finally noticed the mess my parents and their friends had left in the kitchen. There was an empty bowl on the table with crumbs from potato chips. I thought someone had thrown up in it at first, because the bowl was the one we used when we were sick and couldn't make it to the toilet. I'd thrown up in that bowl countless times.

Usually, my parents cleaned up a bit more, but this morning, bottles and cans littered the countertop. Drinking didn't make any sense to me. It was irresponsible. A faint, stale cigarette smell lingered, and the table was sticky with spilled strange liquids. I imagined the adults all sitting around that sticky table, how they laughed and joked and made me cry, and then left a mess for me to look at the next morning.

It wasn't fair.

I went to the living room with my juice box. The sun was rising and beginning to shine on the closed curtains, which made them glow. The coloring book I was working on was from the newest Disney movie, *Enchanted*. I was committed to coloring every page in the book in order, and so I went to find it and continue my thrilling creative journey.

Coloring books were amazing because I got to be artistic without having to do much imagining. It was creativity but with rules I already understood. Instead of the busy, fast feeling of my brain, which was going even faster because of the mess and the juice box and the sticky counter, the coloring was quiet. It allowed my brain to focus on one thing only and settle. I colored everything correctly: the sky blue, the tomato red, the crocodile green, and so on. Everything was colored as it was in life, and that made it good.

I never allowed anyone else to color in my coloring pages, as mine were always better than theirs. Mine were better because I followed the rules. It was wrong to color the stem of a flower pink, but people liked to do stupid things like that sometimes. I had no idea why. It was yet another example of how others seemed to understand a world that I didn't. It made no sense to me to color anything other than the true colors I saw.

If other people couldn't follow the rules, they weren't allowed to play with my things.

So, no one was allowed to touch my stuff. Not anyone.

Not even Graham. He was the worst, because he was five. He was messy. He didn't color in the lines. He used any colors he wanted.

I opened the curtains to see cows outside in the farmyard and the field, and to light the living room so I could look for my coloring book. I didn't have to look far because it was on the floor in front of the window.

My coloring books were not supposed to be out on the floor; they had a special place in a bin that went under the coffee table, and the markers were kept there too. But now my markers were not in their case in the proper order. Some were laid out on the floor, and the book was open.

Detective Paige

If I had been sleepwalking, I would still be incapable of causing this disaster.

This meant that I hadn't done this.

Someone else had opened my coloring book.

Someone else had flipped to a page in my coloring book that was not ready to be colored.

Someone colored in my coloring book.

Someone colored the princess dress a completely wrong color with my markers, then didn't put them back in their case.

My eyes darted around the page, noticing everything they did wrong. My brain ping-ponged, a table tennis ball bouncing around in there, out of control.

The princess's skin was too orange. Ping-pong.

The picture wasn't even complete. Ping-pong.

They went over the lines. Her hair was supposed to be brown. The picture wasn't supposed to be colored yet. Ping-pong. Ping-pong.

One of my parents' friends must've found my coloring books while I was sleeping. She decided to color and sign the page, like she thought it would be a gift to me. She thought I would be happy and think that she'd done a nice thing. My parents let her, knowing full well how I'd react.

This was a problem my brain needed solved.

Dilemma

- I couldn't leave the page inside the book. I hadn't colored it, and it was colored incorrectly, and there were pages in front of it that needed to be colored first. It couldn't just stay there, ruining everything.

- I couldn't rip the page out. I had wanted to color *this* page eventually. I couldn't cheat and pretend like the page never existed, because then I would never color the whole book. I'd feel guilty for ripping it out, and I'd never want to color in the book ever again. I couldn't leave it, but I couldn't make it go away.

So, I grabbed Wite-Out. I sat with the tiny spongy paintbrush, trying to squish liquid paper inside the lines of the princess dress, crying over how imperfect the whole situation was, and crying harder when my coloring over the Wite-Out didn't stay and looked worse. My hands were shaking and my vision was blurry because I was sobbing so hard, kneeling on the floor, dizzy and distressed.

My face was over my ruined coloring book, which was now coated in tears as well as Wite-Out. I was unable to get the straw through my grape juice box.

I finally gave up.

I didn't want to bother my family with my crying, and my chest was choking with my fat tears. Sobbing, I tried to put the markers back in their case, but couldn't remember the order because I only ever took one out at a time so I would never mess it up. I'd never had to think about it before. The markers would forever be ruined, just like my book.

Insights

If only I hadn't gone to sleep. If only I'd taken all my things into my room. My parents knew that I didn't want anyone to color in my book. They let that happen. They didn't think it was as serious as I did. I didn't know how to make them see my world. I was alone.

I'd never asked for this life and I didn't want to do it anymore. I wasn't going to survive if I had to live like this, where every little thing out of place created stress and anxiety. It was too hard, too difficult to accommodate. And it seemed like it'd never end.

Conclusion

One day, I'll be big. Then I will be strong enough to make myself stop living.

I can't wait to stop living.

When I was eight, these feelings of wanting to die grew enough that I wrote a suicide letter. I didn't know what to do with it. I was filled with guilt and pain. Being how I was, being so different, and not knowing how to ask for help made everything harder.

The letter was filled with apologies and practical details. It informed my family who I wanted to give my stuff to.

I hid the letter in my closet. I thought about it constantly. It burned in my brain; those words became the picture I saw. The very existence of the letter made me feel guilty. To try to assuage the guilt, a few weeks after I wrote it, I showed it to my mom.

She was sitting on her bed and I passed her the letter. I bawled my eyes out.

She became very still, holding the letter. "Alright," she said. "I'm sorry you feel like this. The things you're upset about aren't as big of a deal as you think. That's no reason to kill yourself."

Her words tumbled out and over me.

"I'm sorry. I know it's a lot," I said. "It's just how I feel."

"That's a lot to feel," she said. Her voice was quiet. She stayed on the bed, holding the letter, looking at me like she was waiting for me to say something to make this all better.

"I want the letter destroyed," I said. "It scares me."

"I'll take this to work and shred it," she said.

"Supper's ready," Dad called from the kitchen.

We left the conversation awkwardly and without a conclusion. I followed her out of the room to our family supper table. I ate in silence, without looking at anyone. I was the first to finish dinner most days, not liking to dillydally with chitchat, and today was no different. I ate, asked to be excused, and cleared the table, then I went to my room. There was nothing else to say.

CHAPTER 6

DEEPER MEANING

other people

i look like other people
i can act like other people
i am not like other people
why? how?

GRADUATED GRADE SIX AND WENT TO MIDDLE SCHOOL FOR grades seven and eight, leaving Graham and my old school behind. I was excited because several schools congregated into this middle school, and I was hoping that finally I'd meet more people like me.

I've never been afraid of meeting new people.

A new person is a new opportunity

They have no expectations or an opinion about me yet.

They're a chance to learn about a different life and a different world. They have new perspectives.

Maybe they have really good ideas.

Maybe they'll end up becoming my best friend.

Maybe we're soulmates or twin flames.

The bus stopped at the middle school first, so I got off before Graham. He was for sure fine without me, and I was going to be fine without him. I felt a little sad about it, but I was his big sister so I walked down the aisle with purpose. I was a big kid, and I sat at the back of the bus now. The very back seat on the left. The day before, I'd spent hours trying to plan the perfect outfit. My stomach hurt all morning. And my heart was racing, but I didn't want Graham to see how worried I was about my new venture.

"Have fun! Good luck!" Graham shouted. He hugged me as I reached his seat. Some of the little kids on the bus stood up and added to the hug Graham already formed around me, little kids who I knew from school. Lots of the kids in the younger grades knew me to sit at the front of the bus with them, talk to them, and tell them stories. Last year, I was a bus buddy for a younger girl, Deina. I helped her pack up at the end of the day and listened to her chatter about her thoughts and her life. I adored her. I sang to her on the bus and couldn't wait to meet her little sister when she started school that year. I hugged all the kids back, and told them I was going to miss them too. I squeezed Deina tightest.

I was going to be okay, for her, for all of them.

One. Two. Three. Four steps down off the bus.

I arrived at the tall, old, red-brick building with anticipation. The front doors were huge, and although they weren't used, I liked how they appeared. I looked around to see if there was anyone I knew. Some girls from my old school were in a little group, standing by a tree in front of those large doors. I could tell they were nervous, too, in the way that they were huddled together with shifting feet. I skipped toward them and smiled as I approached.

A girl I knew who always had messy hair turned to me and smiled. "This is my friend Sam. She's from up north."

Sam was taller than me, with a long, oval face framed by straight, red hair. She had a very symmetrical face and freckled skin. She spoke like she was kind and welcoming, and she invited me to walk with her to homeroom. We sat together in the front.

Ms. Dales, our homeroom teacher, walked in with a shaky smile and red cheeks. She was just over five feet tall but looked taller in heels that clicked on the hardwood floors. She had light blonde hair and bangs and glasses, soft features, and a kind smile. If she dressed differently, she could've been confused for a student. She was young; I believe in her late twenties. I could see she was sweating, and her hands didn't seem to know where to go. She smiled, but only briefly, then resumed talking while taking short breaths and pacing in front of us.

She seemed nervous, which made me curious.

FIELD NOTES

It is not good behavior to be nervous when you're in charge. I wonder if the class will see her negatively.

Ms. Dales started off by introducing herself. "I'm new to having my own homeroom here. I was a French teacher before. My previous French students made fun of me because I wore black every single day, and so I wanted to shake it up for you and wear a pink dress today."

It was the only time we saw her in color.

FIELD NOTES

It's more okay to be nervous when you do something for the first time.

Ms. Dales was also there for the first time; that meant she understood how I felt. That made me feel different, but a good different. I felt relief and comfort knowing that she didn't have expectations of me. If she was nervous, maybe I could be too.

At twelve years old, I constantly compared myself to others. I watched how people behaved and then watched how other people around them reacted to that behavior. If the reaction was positive, then I thought that behavior was good and adopted it. If the reaction was negative, I figured the behavior was bad and made a mental note to never act that way.

BEHAVIOR	REACTION	WHAT I'M GOING TO DO
Being an extrovert	Finds friends easily	Be more extroverted
Looking people in the eye	People paid attention more	Look in people's eyes. Try to blink more.
Sharing belongings	People seem happy and build trust	I could **not** share my belongings. No. I could try my best.
Talking back to the teacher	Students and the teacher seemed to find this disrespectful	I won't do this. It is not a good way to make friends.

My list of Acquired Human Knowledge helped me feel prepared for middle school. Among all the new middle school students, I knew what to do. And I had Sam, sitting right next to me, navigating all of this at my side.

Teachers were hit-or-miss. I had a hard time treating authority figures like they were above me, as I did not believe that they were. I believed that people were people, and just because someone is older and in charge of me doesn't mean anything else. If I thought an idea was dumb, I wouldn't follow it. If I thought someone was being disrespectful, I probably wouldn't respect them. I didn't suck up to anybody, but I especially didn't suck up to teachers—unless they made me feel good and I wanted them to also feel good as natural reciprocity of respect and admiration.

Some teachers really didn't like me, and I thought it was because I questioned them. I questioned everything. To my mind, teachers *knew*. That was the point! That was their job! I couldn't handle a teacher being wrong, because why would anyone want to be wrong? Shouldn't it be the teacher's job to teach everything correctly? I could never let even the smallest mistake go unnoticed. I had to correct the teacher so the students would have the right answers. It was only fair. *Someone* had to do things properly.

I only wanted to find the truth. I never really understood that there was a certain curriculum and that school was only for learning it. I was the kid who sat at the front of the room and constantly had their hand up:

- To answer
- To correct the teacher
- To ask for a different explanation

Everyone else seemed to understand what a teacher initially taught. I did not. So, I tried to associate the information with something that I *did* understand. Then I asked if my understanding was correct based on that.

Most people looked at what was in front of them for clues and then worked their way to becoming more specific until they reached an answer. If they saw a futon for the first time, they began piecing it together by noticing that it had attributes of a couch and of a bed. Then, they could understand how the never-before-seen object (futon) was intended to be used based on what they knew about couches and beds.

My brain didn't work like that. It started specifically and then checked my memory to figure out if I had seen it before in order to know how it worked. My brain didn't see a futon and think it was kind of like a couch or kind of like a bed. It wasn't a couch or a bed, and my brain wouldn't put it in either category because my brain was specific. A futon was a futon and functioned as a futon, which is separate from a bed or a couch. When we had to put things into categories, I had a hard time finding connections, because my brain was always zoomed in like that.

For the previous eight years of school, none of my classmates had complained that I annoyed or bothered them with my questions. I hadn't even noticed that I asked a lot of them. I didn't feel embarrassed to have my hand raised and initiate a one-on-one conversation with the teacher. I wanted answers. I needed to understand in order to know how to use the information.

I deeply wished I could understand the way it seemed everyone else could. And I wished that when people explained information to me, I didn't have to question it and look at it eighteen different ways before I could process it correctly.

I knew my lack of understanding cost a lot of time in class, as the teacher had to pause to explain. The teachers who were frustrated and impatient were the ones I asked even more questions, because I got flustered and more confused.

It all became a very slippery slope, one that often left me crying and, even though I didn't know it at the time, burned out. My brain felt tired and unable to process new information or do anything other than work on surviving.

My tears frustrated some teachers even *more*. I sat at the front of the class, trying really hard not to make loud noises as I cried.

Soon, I stopped raising my hand because I was unable to speak. Sam put her hand up to ask a question. Or to give an answer. She knew a lot of what I wanted to ask and tried to help.

We wanted to make our homeroom teacher, Ms. Dales, happy because she was so lovely to us. We wanted to be a really good class for her, and for all the teachers and principals to think she was the best. Universally, we loved her.

Ms. Dales was a teacher who liked me. It didn't take long for her to know the way I was, especially with my education. She was a good teacher, not only because she was a good person but because she was skilled at explanations. If I couldn't grasp a concept, she tried to work with my brain to find a way to make the idea click. She saw how I struggled when I didn't understand, and I think she didn't want me to feel like that if she could help. She knew what made me frustrated and was usually able to stop me from spiraling.

I always tried to watch myself. I didn't want to get frustrated with her. I didn't want to raise my voice or have a pointed tone or become mean or angry by accident. I respected Ms. Dales a lot, and I also knew that she was a very sensitive person, like I was. I never wanted to make her feel any sort of negative way. I never wanted her to think that I thought of her in a negative way either. If I did get frustrated and snippy, I made a point of apologizing later, explaining myself, and mending our personal relationship.

Everyone who I spent time with, including Sam, had their own groups of friends. When it came to lunchtime, we had to go to one of the lunchrooms and stay there. I clung to Sam's side and joined her and the friends she'd already made. I tried to talk to them too. When they asked questions and I responded, they looked me up and down and ignored me. The ball of conversation, as soon as it got to me, deflated. I couldn't understand why. The girls talked among each other, and rumors got around that they didn't like me. I felt like I hadn't done anything to them to deserve that. It was hard to find friends. Groups started to form, and when I tried to come into those groups, people acted weirdly, as if they wanted me to go away. Sam started to get busy with sports at lunch, and I didn't do sports, so I had to find somewhere else to go. I tried to sign up for clubs so that my lunch and recess hours would be covered, and I wouldn't have to guess where I was going to have lunch that day. And I wouldn't have to choose a different seat every day.

I became very close with Ms. Dales. Over the course of middle school, she became someone I confided in. She stayed in her classroom with me at lunch, so I could eat with her and not be alone. I liked the appearance of choosing to be alone rather than just happening to be alone. While I liked being by myself, feeling alone in a school full of middle school kids didn't feel good. At all. I couldn't wander around optionless. I needed to know where my seat was, and that wasn't safe with students because I didn't have a spot. But I did with Ms. Dales.

Ms. Dales was the person I ran to, crying, because a teacher yelled at me or I felt things were unfair in the world or in school or I had a crush on a boy that was really bothering me or I was so frustrated with my brain. We shared stories about ourselves and how we viewed the world and other people.

I think we trusted each other. I know that I trusted her. Everyone thought Ms. Dales was really freaking cool, so I didn't get made fun of for having a teacher as a best friend. Everyone wanted to be best friends with Ms. Dales, so I was just the lucky one. I connected well with her and felt like I related to her better than I did to the other kids, although I always had Sam.

Ms. Dales accommodated and accepted me and wanted to help me. She did her best, and that was more than most people. I'll always be thankful for that.

Thoughts

In English class, specifically in deciphering a "deeper meaning" within a text, it is difficult because I have to answer, "How smart do you think this author is?" There are not that many people who are smart enough to make every single word in a novel or a script relevant. Have you watched screenwriters answer theories from fans? Most of the time I see them, they're like, "Oh. Mm. That's a coincidence. Cool idea, though. We shoulda went with that."

In grade seven, Ms. Dales also taught English. I had trouble with English sometimes. I didn't understand some concepts. English was either really easy or really hard, and it differed each day.

We had one project where we had to pick a song and write an essay explaining the deeper themes and meanings in the lyrics. The song was supposed to be metaphorical, representing a grander overall message.

I wasn't good at finding the deeper meaning. I didn't assume an author meant one thing if they said another. I thought that was quite useless. I noticed this analysis was implemented in class sometimes, but I always thought people were just guessing. In my reality, no one could ever be correct in their explanation, because only the author would know what they really meant. And I thought it was redundant to question what someone meant, when they said what they said. It frustrated me, because if the author did mean something other than what they had written, that meant that they were lying to me. And I couldn't tell when someone was lying to me.

I took books literally. I enjoyed book after book for years and *never* thought there were hidden layers. I enjoyed books as they were, like I thought I was supposed to. I didn't know I was supposed to dig deeper for themes and metaphors and subtle lessons.

The original song I chose for the essay for Ms. Dales was "Mean" by Taylor Swift. I thought it would be a good one because in the first line Taylor compares words to knives and swords and weapons, which was a simile, which was kind of like a metaphor, which was kind of the whole point of this project.

Quotes from the song and their "deeper meaning" that I came up with

- "Words like knives and swords and weapons": Words hurt.
- "Wildfire lies": Lies spread like wildfire.
- "Somebody made you cold": They weren't actually cold temperature-wise, but it was another way to say that they weren't loving or caring.

- "Big enough so you can't hit me": either (a) you can't hit
  someone you can't reach, or (b) if you hit someone who is a lot
  bigger than you, they probably won't feel it as a hit and may
  think you tickled them instead

Ms. Dales vetoed the song. "You might have a hard time analyzing for deeper meanings because it's pretty shallow."

"Shallow?" I repeated.

"Yes. Why don't we try something else?" She smiled at me.

"I don't know a good one to choose."

"Let's try 'The Times They Are A-Changin' by Bob Dylan." She tidied some papers from her desk. "That song would provide a lot of material to analyze." She looked up at me.

"Okay." I relinquished control. I had to because I didn't understand. And it felt numb.

Quotes from the song and their "deeper meaning" that I came up with

- "Admit that the waters around you have grown": Water grows? Or something?
- "For the loser now will be later to win": People don't lose all of the time. Sometimes you win, and you may win later.
- "For he that gets hurt will be he who has stalled": You don't want to waste your time and procrastinate.
- "If your time to you is worth savin', then you better start swimmin' or you'll sink like a stone": LIKE A STONE. Simile.

I worked in the computer lab with the other kids. It was peaceful in there, and we could type our essays. Ms. Dales spent her time quietly chatting with a couple of the other students who had difficulty typing or had trouble with essays or weren't the best at staying focused.

I was independent, and Ms. Dales knew that. Everyone knew Paige did not need, nor did she want, any project to be a collaboration.

But that day, working on my essay, Ms. Dales stayed by me.

"What do you think about this line?" she asked. "You could go a little deeper here," she added and pointed at the notes I'd made.

I stared at the lyrics and waited for more meaning to jump out. We never learned *how* to find deeper meanings, so I didn't have a set of rules to follow. I had no idea how to move forward. How was everyone else able to do this task? I couldn't figure out how to interpret the song as a single whole.

She tilted her head. "Hmmmm. How about how the rain represents the sad, somber tone of the song?" she asked. "Don't you think it does that?"

Rain was sad and somber in this song? I didn't think so. I liked the rain.

a mess with her

rain talks, roars, whispers,
she screams
cries of peace, cries that can sound like rebellion,
anarchy, with the footsteps that run to take shelter,
their parade floats and wedding dresses drenched.

but, i welcome her to pour on top of my picnics,
take my human life and rinse it of its significance,
thrash my face and dampen my socks
without wrath, without love, without needing to need
to acknowledge me at all.

make a mess,
in abundance or frequency, i could not care.

> *i will always feel compelled to put on my rain jacket,*
> *and go outside to sing along with the birds,*
> *and be a mess with you.*

> ~ do you notice how the sky changes color when you
> leave?

"No," I replied. "Why is rain supposed to mean sad and somber? I enjoy the rain. Rain is not sad and somber to me. Icy snow is sad and somber. Can I say that if a song talks about icy snow, or do I have to make a rule that rain is supposed to mean sad and somber in writing?"

I didn't wait to listen to a response from Ms. Dales, because I knew there wasn't a simple answer. I shut down. I spent my time in the computer lab staring at the screen with silent tears rolling down my face.

- My thoughts were wrong.
- That meant they were invalid and they should be thrown in the trash.
- I did not know why I was wrong, but most importantly, I didn't know what I could even do to be right.

Ms. Dales was just as confused as I was. I rarely struggled with work once I understood the rules and those rules were seemingly straight-forward. I didn't know what to do, and she didn't know how to help.

I didn't finish the essay. I jotted down ideas about the song, but it was not an essay and didn't dive deeper into its meaning. I handed it in anyway, ashamed and embarrassed. It felt like I'd let my teacher down. Now she had to read my pitiful work and feel bad as she failed me. I couldn't look her in the eye for days afterward because I didn't want to see her upset with me or disappointed. I told my mom about this, and she told me, "You're doing great. Don't worry. You're so smart, smarter than your dad or I ever were. I don't know why you're complaining. I don't know what you're upset about."

Questions
Were authors not just recounting events but using underlying meaning and saying more than just the words the whole time?
   Had I read every book wrong?

I couldn't stop thinking about the project until we got our grades back. Ms. Dales walked around handing back everyone's paper except mine. "Paige?" she asked. "Could you come out to the hallway to speak privately?"

I started to cry before I even made my way out of the room. I didn't know exactly what she was going to say, but it was going to be awful. I thought maybe she would show me my grade away from the other students because she knew I would cry and panic and she didn't want me to be embarrassed, or maybe she was going to say that my work was pitiful and she didn't even read it and I actually was going to fail grade seven and she hated me and I was a bad kid because I didn't work hard enough.

None of that happened.

Ms. Dales told me she wasn't going to give my essay back, so I would never see my grade. She also said she hadn't submitted it, so we were just going to pretend like it had never happened, and it wouldn't affect anything at all.

I hugged her and cried for too long, filled with relief. I felt so awful for making Ms. Dales deal with all of that without me learning anything or achieving anything. I was happy and thankful it was done and over and okay.

We didn't know why I had such a hard time.

Ms. Dales showed me that sometimes you could even the playing field. She cared about my struggles and my differences and wanted to make things fair. I couldn't believe it. She made me realize that I could not be perfect all the time and it doesn't have to matter. She did something she wasn't really allowed to, because she saw that the project wasn't right for me.

English class got harder and harder. I read books quickly, so any assigned reading, I completed before it was due. There were checkpoints along the way: every Friday, Ms. Dales read aloud the chapter we were supposed to be on, and then we would discuss it. I didn't like listening to anyone read. I felt a quiet but sharp and intense burn inside of my stomach whenever:

- A word was fumbled
- Time needed to be taken to figure out how to pronounce the word
- A word was skipped
- A word was pronounced improperly
- The punctuation wasn't followed
- The rhythm and inflections were off
- Someone took too long flipping the page

I didn't get mad or do anything when it happened. I just felt the fire burn quietly inside me. I tried not to listen to anyone read out loud, because it bothered me so much. I distracted myself by doodling little flowers on my paper, or making paper cranes out of sticky notes, or I just silently read ahead wherever I was and used that as free time.

Less fire.

When we discussed a chapter as a class, I felt very confident in the material to be able to participate in the discussion. I recalled everything that happened.

One day, Ms. Dales asked, "How did Mariah *feel* when she gave her speech?"

I raised my hand. "She said she felt excited and confident."

"Yep. What else is she feeling?"

What else? I didn't know. I looked through my book to find the line I must have missed.

The character didn't say how she felt anywhere else in the chapter, I was sure of it.

That's when someone who usually didn't know the answer raised their hand and said, "She also felt nervous and stressed out."

"Why?" Ms. Dales asked.

Yeah, why? That was clearly wrong, because those words were never in the book.

"'Cause her hands were all slippery, and she felt dizzy and shaky and almost like throwing up."

What?

"Absolutely," Ms. Dales replied, smiling.

What? No—

"Anything else?"

WHAT? There was MORE? No, no, wait—

"I think after, she felt pretty sad about everything."

No, no. How did you—

The discussion kept on going without me, but I raised my hand hard to interrupt and ask a question. I waited until prompted. In my inside world, everything stopped, and there was only this question.

"How do you know that, though?" I asked.

"Know what?" Ms. Dales asked.

"Know how she felt."

"Well, we can't say for sure, but we can make *inferences* from the text. Read between the lines."

There is nothing to read between the *lines of text*. Why not just read what is meant to be read and interpret that? "How," I asked slowly, "do you read between the lines?"

"You kind of just . . . take what is said and pretend like it's you. Does that make sense?"

"No."

"So, if your hands were all slippery and wet, and you were dizzy and shaking and felt like throwing up, how do you think you'd feel?"

There are so many different reasons. Your hands could be wet and slippery from water or oil or Vaseline. The character could've been dizzy because she hadn't eaten anything all day and had low blood sugar. Maybe she was shaking because she was cold. And maybe she felt like throwing up because she ate some bad food and is getting sick, or got poisoned or something. "How do you tell which feeling it is?"

"It's the most obvious one."

But it's not obvious to me, is it?

I vowed to figure out why I couldn't grasp deeper meanings in songs or books. I needed to make sure it wasn't just because I hadn't worked hard enough. I looked and looked, and I tried so hard to analyze texts at home. I googled analyses of other songs . . . and it didn't change anything. No amount of practice or research made me understand.

I promised myself I was going to find out why. But, honestly, the result of all this was that I fell off from reading fiction in my free time after we started breaking it down in school. It made me realize that there was so much more to these stories—which I loved so much and thought I knew so well—that I didn't read at all.

I was just . . . reading wrong. I was devastated. I felt like I'd been lied to.

FIELD NOTES

This is hard.
All the time.

CHAPTER 7

MAYBE WE'RE TWIN FLAMES

core

all my years of masking
presenting a beautifully decorated and heavily reinforced
shell,
with what inside?

IN GRADE SEVEN, I WAS PICKED ON BY A GROUP OF GIRLS WHO SPE-
cifically said I was "too happy, too smiley, too skippy, too preppy."
I didn't understand. I still don't understand. However, one of those
girls is my best friend now (she never said nasty stuff to me, so we
were cool). A decade later, she told me something that blew my
mind. When I asked her about that time of our lives and her opinion of me, she recalled her experience and why she didn't like me so
much.

"It was like you were a doll. You were smiling and talking on
the outside, but when I looked at you, I felt like there was nothing
inside."

I remembered grade seven and how empty I felt, and I said, "Oh
my god."

"Like you were programmed. Like you were a shell of a person, but there wasn't a 'Paige' in there. You just seemed very fake. Uncanny valley vibes for real."

"Oh my *god* dude . . . I didn't know I was autistic then . . . I was masking . . . You were *right*. I was *literally* a shell of a person."

"*Wait*, do you think that's what it is?"

I was in tears. That perspective showed me the result of all my years of masking. Going back to that time of my life is painful. Every day was a challenge. But there were a few people who made it less difficult, who walked beside me as I stumbled.

My friend Sam was really important to me during these years. She did a lot of activities outside of school and kept herself busy and evolving. Recently, she'd joined a dance studio in town and took some recreational classes and had really liked it.

"Do you want to come to dance class with me?" Sam asked as we walked out of class one day. She took long strides, strong and straight, while I skipped next to her, bouncing loosely and without a pattern. She was a sturdy maypole that grounded my dancing ribbon. But I had quit dance when I was six. The teacher was always yelling and I cried all class, panicking. That teacher made my brain feel scattered. She wasn't good at explaining, and I couldn't ask the right questions to get her to explain any differently. She was insensitive and rude and loud. Other kids cried too. But I didn't want to quit dance when I was thirteen.

"I don't know," I said.

"I think you'd like it."

"I'll be behind everyone else."

"We would be there together," she said, smiling. "I've only been going under a year. You can already do the splits. You'll catch up really fast."

I knew if Sam felt happy and confident there, then maybe she could help show me how to feel the same. After a year or two of dance, as we developed into our own dancers and began to get comfortable in our bodies, we differentiated a bit in styles: Sam took more to hip-hop, and I took more to contemporary. I actually really took to it. I also really liked helping the younger kids at the studio. They got excited when they saw me and had to come say hi. I explained concepts to them and helped with their technique. I was completely myself around kids, and they liked me for who I was.

Rules of the body
I always felt like I could dance. When I saw dancers, I thought, I could do that too. If someone just told me how to move and when, I could make my body do it, easily. And then when I started, it was true. I loved dancing on my own anyway, I was already quite flexible, and I noticed I looked kind of pretty. I moved all of the time, always skipping or bouncing or nodding or swaying. I didn't know I could move so beautifully. It became a hyperfocus. A discipline.

Sam's motivation was always to do well, be kind, polite, and courteous. She never gave anything less than her best. She was very family oriented, with a huge motivation to protect and care for her younger sister, who was in Graham's year. She got good grades, she was incredibly athletic, she sang and danced and had a character that not one person spoke poorly about—at least not out loud. She was kind, quiet, and modest, but she was also a lot of fun. She was hilariously witty and quick, and she knew when I was sarcastic and when I was serious. She laughed at just about anything I did or said.

She always got asked if she played volleyball or basketball because she was built tall and strong, and she did. She also played soccer, badminton, track and field, dance, and more. She volunteered around town with different churches and nonprofits. She sang in choir and played the piano and the clarinet. A lot came naturally and easily to her, but Sam never wanted to be the star of the show. She didn't need praise or recognition, and in fact was quite embarrassed by it. She had the energy and the drive and the talent to pursue whatever she wanted, so she did. That's all she needed.

I took pride in how easily I could make her laugh. Her humor was serious and logical and played within the rules.

She was supportive and caring and kind above all else. Even with all of her many talents and accomplishments, she made anyone feel like the world was on their side. Sam could convince anyone that they were capable of doing anything perfectly.

We liked to sit in the front of the class. It was better, and we made a list as to why.

- Less in field of view meant fewer distractions.
- Visual and auditory optimization: the board was clearest to see without obstruction, and it was the best place to hear the teacher.
- I was held accountable by being in the teacher's line of sight.
- No one behind me could see my face, so they didn't see me cry.
- I couldn't see who raised their hand, who rolled their eyes, who giggled.

Sam was okay with adding those last few points, even when they didn't affect her. I didn't have to try to be friends with her, or try to impress her, like I did with everyone else. She was really special because she chose me as her friend for who I was. Everyone loved her and wanted to be near her. One night at dance, a girl who was ten years younger than us, Bella, was going to do a duet with one of the older girls, whichever older girl she picked and got along with best. A lot of the dancers at the studio thought she'd pick Sam, because of her demeanor. I just smiled. I had a feeling Bella would pick me. Girls our age really liked Sam, but girls Bella's age really liked me. It wasn't long before Bella became my mini-me.

After school one day, I stayed in town instead of going on the bus home. I sat in a booth at Burger King in the mall with a couple of other people from class. They were chatting together as I sat and ate my french fries. I faced the doors that led to outside, and I could see the Sport Chek store across the hall. A guy walked into the mall with someone who looked like she was probably his mother. He was taller, but they had similar faces: round, blue eyes, full cheeks, and the same perfect teeth.

He recognized the people I sat with. As soon as he made eye contact, he bounced over to our booth and sat down across from me without being invited. His mother walked into Sport Chek without him. He introduced himself.

"Hey, I'm Max."

He was undeniably attractive, with his perfect smile and naturally muscular arms. He stood half a foot taller than the crowd and spoke half an octave deeper. He looked like a sixteen-year-old. "And, who are you?" he said to me, looking straight into my eyes. He had noticeable light-blue eyes that popped against his tan.

"I'm Paige," I said. I smiled without blinking.

"Paige, eh?" He lifted his right hand above the table, as if to shake mine. No one had done that before to me, and I liked it. I kept my smile and grabbed his hand, shaking it firmly. I don't always like touching other people, or when other people touch me, but this had a start and end, and a purpose. It was controlled. From this point on, I shook people's hands during introductions.

"Whoa, strong grip. I like that," he said.

I rolled my eyes and giggled a little. I didn't know I had a strong grip. I didn't know I liked it when strangers pointed out traits they noticed about my authentic self. Our friends continued talking, and we listened in on the conversation.

He stared back at me after a while. "You're beautiful," he said.

"Thanks," I said and looked away. I could feel that he didn't look away.

"Do you want my number?" he asked.

What? "No," I replied.

"No?" he said.

The group heard and stopped talking.

"No, thanks," I clarified.

He looked appalled and checked to see if his friends reacted the same. They didn't.

A couple of them said, "Oohhhhh," at Max getting turned down.

This made him a little embarrassed, I could tell. His ears turned red.

When I first met Max that day, I thought he was so confident and cocky. He seemed to be one of those boys who flirted with as many girls as possible without making any real commitment. I saw right through him. I saw something catch in his throat behind his smirk. He looked at me with a filter covering his eyes, and I saw that it was a facade. He was playing a part. He learned a role. He was hiding.

He'd been through a lot, and it was noticeable in the way we connected. I won't share Max's story; that's his. What's important for my story about him is that he noticed subtleties in other people and changed to cater to their emotional needs. Somewhere, he learned to be something, so other people would like him. That was how he learned to be human.

I didn't swoon for him. I found him annoying and boring because he didn't say anything authentic and raw and real.

He demanded attention while at the same time he was absolutely terrified that too much attention would reveal his true self. I didn't fall for his act, and that confused him. It rattled him. That day at the Burger King, he recited his number to me. I memorized it easily, without even intending to. I messaged him randomly one day—we spent so much casual time together that eventually it felt like a natural way to continue our conversation.

For the next year and a half, he showered me in cute text messages and came up to me in the hall or at a sporting event or whenever he possibly could. He tried to schmooze his way into my heart.

One day, he yelled, "Hey, baby girl!" across the hall at me, making my face turn beet red as I rolled my eyes at him. "Looking fine as always, Paigey-Poo."

I shook my head lightly. "Do you say one thing that you made up in your own head?" I asked. "Or is it just pickup lines you read from Instagram?"

"What?" He folded his arms across his chest.

"Where are your real, authentic, valuable thoughts and feelings? Who *are* you, Max Miller?"

"You wanna know who I am?"

Of course I did. He was a very psychologically interesting human, facade or not. He was also very nice to me, facade or not.

"I just want *you* to know who you are."

An OVERWHELMING need for perfection

whatever that was, whatever everyone thought it was I was
determined to find it and *be* perfect.

there just seemed to be never-ending contradictions to every
rule.

if there are contradictions to every rule then how is anything
a rule?

when to use the rule and when the contradiction to the rule?

teachers can be so vague sometimes, especially with subjects
like english and history.

i became overwhelmed when looking at a test question,
knowing i knew the answer but couldn't find it just at that
moment.

or, when i just couldn't figure it out, even though i was sure i
didn't miss anything. even questions worth half a mark.

tears bubbled up and out of me.

when i received a marked test back, i checked over every
single mark and made sure they marked my paper correctly. even
half marks.

i never meant to cry. i never wanted to cry or get frustrated.

some tests i refused to look at upon return, for fear of what
the outcome may do to my mental health.

The bus ride was one of my favorite moments in my day. Deina, the
little girl from my primary school, sometimes joined me at the back
of the bus, or I sat at the front of the bus with her and her sister,
Mya. Those two munchkins encapsulated my forty-five-minute bus
ride to and from school for those years. I loved sitting with them,
singing to them and telling them stories and hearing how funny
they were.

When I graduated grade eight, I was going to be put on another
bus route for my new school, high school. I'd been on that same
bus route since the beginning. Out of everything that changed
about school, the bus route never had. But it was going to, and there
weren't going to be little kids on the bus anymore, just high school-
ers, and I would be the littlest kid, probably.

On the last day of school, on our way home, I noticed some kids
didn't get dropped off at their spot, instead staying on as the bus
pushed forward. I said to the driver, who was now a woman called
Sandy, "I think you missed a stop!"

"Oh, did I?" she replied, and grinned at me in the mirror.

All the kids were grinning at me, I realized. The next stop was
mine, and as we approached, I saw my driveway was filled with cars
and parents who climbed up onto the bus to give me presents and
wish me a happy grad. This moment made such an imprint on my
soul. The look on all of the kids' faces when they waited to see my

reaction is something I'll never forget. They smiled at me with gratitude and love.

I ugly cried.

The valedictorian in most schools was usually the student at the top of the class, and I wished we did it that way. But at our school, the graduating grade eight class voted for their valedictorian representative, based off the teachers' recommendations. I was upset about that, because I really wanted to be valedictorian and I was top of the class. I loved speeches, and I was good at giving them, but I wasn't sure if my peers would vote for me. The teachers selected three students to put on the ballot for valedictorian; my name was one! Every grade eight kid had to vote. I waited for the result, unsure if I would be picked. But I was. *Phew.*

After my teacher told me I was valedictorian, I told her I wanted to keep it a secret and not tell *anyone.* Not Sam. Not Graham. I didn't even tell my parents. The goal was, at the time of the valedictorian address, I would rise from the bench and the crowd would erupt into thunderous applause as the secret was revealed (if they didn't already read ahead in the program).

I love surprises, which is surprising in and of itself. But people are made up of contradictions, and while I love to know what's happening (like with my bologna sandwich), I also love a good surprise.

A teacher from my school, Mr. Lowell, saw my dad at a baseball practice the day before graduation. He had no idea I planned to keep being valedictorian a secret, so he accidentally let the cat out of the bag. He said to my dad at baseball, "You must be so proud of Paige."

"Uh, yeah, sure? Always?" Dad said, apparently.

"Y'know, 'cause she's valedictorian."

Dad, of course, did not know this.

The next day, Mr. Lowell came up to me as all 137 of us sat in rows in front of the stage in the gym. We practiced walking on and off the stage, and now it was time to practice sitting still for a useless amount of time.

"Paige!" he whispered. He snuck forward and sat in a chair in the row in front of me, facing backward. He was a very well-liked teacher. He was young and handsome and kind and patient and apparently a wonderful teacher—*and* he taught math, which was the best subject. Plus, he played baseball with my dad, so I felt comfortable with him, as if he were another one of my own teachers.

"Mr. Lowell!" I said back, jokingly mimicking his expression.

He smiled, and then his face became a little more serious. "You didn't tell your parents you're valedictorian?"

Three people gasped: me, the girl right next to me, and Sam, who sat in the row behind me.

"Mr. Lowell . . ." I murmured. I was so disappointed! My hard work! My secrets! I only had a few hours left!

"Paige! That's amazing!" Sam beamed from behind me before I could reply. She stood up and wrapped her arms around my neck. "Why didn't you tell me?!" She smushed her cheek against the side of my forehead. I crossed my arms to touch hers and reciprocate the neck hug while I blushed and smiled at Mr. Lowell.

"I didn't tell *anyone*," I said. One little tear came in my eye and I tried to smile it away. I rubbed Sam's arms. My hands were sweaty and we both realized that at the same time.

Mr. Lowell was embarrassed. "Oh, Paige! I'm so sorry . . ." His eyes darted around me at the faces looking. Only a few of my classmates heard, but one of the most important ones was one of them.

Sam buffered for me by talking to Mr. Lowell while I looked at the ceiling and tried to suck the tears back in through my eyeballs. "C'mon, Mr. Lowell!" I said in a lighthearted, playful way. "You're just ruining it for me everywhere, aren't ya?"

I kept it a secret from everyone else, and when graduation came, it was about as exciting as I imagined when our class looked around to see which one of us was about to stand up and walk to the podium. I didn't have to look at their eyes to know that they were on me as my name was announced. I looked where I was going and smiled confidently and flipped my curled golden hair over my shoulder. Speeches were my shit, and I was so excited to blow it out of the water.

Ms. Dales wasn't my teacher that year, but she was the teacher I took pictures with onstage that night.

We sang with the school choir at the end of the ceremony, Sam and me both. I had a little solo at the beginning with another friend, Juliette, who was younger. Sam came on with the rest of the choir and came up right beside me. I grabbed Juliette's hand, and I grabbed Sam's with two fingers and the microphone. We hugged and cried at the end.

CHAPTER 8
THIS ISN'T NORMAL

their words

a big overachiever. a hard worker. a perfectionist.
a try hard.
but i didn't try hard.
i didn't try.
i did.
i accomplished.
it was not discipline or impulse control or work ethic.
it was panic, escape,
and the only order i've ever known.

SAM AND I WORE THE SAME OUTFIT ON THE FIRST DAY OF GRADE nine. At the high school orientation that took place in the summer before school started, we mapped out the school together. We walked from each other's lockers to each classroom to each bathroom so we knew where to go on our first day. That was something we both got nervous about. We needed to be punctual and in control.

We felt confident getting around on our first day. We gave each other little looks whenever someone arrived late to class because they got lost. *They should've done what we did*, was what we meant.

In Mrs. Larson's grade nine English class, we were assigned to sit in the back, in the far-right corner of the room, next to the Greek mythology posters and the decimated, chipped corkboard. Sam sat behind me, right in that corner. Sam's best subject was English, and my worst subject was English, so it was a mistake for us to be kept in the back, as, for those differing reasons, we were the main participants.

Mrs. Larson had a lot of compassion for me, but she really didn't know what to do with my questions. English only got harder as I got older, and the concepts became more theoretical.

As my frustration increased, so did my persistence in explaining and rewording my explanation, trying to find the golden nugget of information she needed to understand my question. One day, I asked several questions about *To Kill a Mockingbird*.

"Paige, it's seriously not that big of a deal. Let's just keep going," Mrs. Larson said. She pushed her hair back from her face, her cheeks turning red.

"It is a big deal, Mrs. Larson. Is it going to be on the test?"

"I mean . . . probably. I don't know."

"Then it's a big deal and I don't understand it and I really need your help."

On the word "help," my voice turned all the way up on the high-pitched squeakiness knob and I breathed in, quick, sharp, and really loud.

A warm lump sat in my throat and made my eyes bulge with the force of holding it all in. I tried to speak and my voice cracked, and some of the class turned around. I knew they were looking to see if I was going to cry. A couple of girls at the front nudged each other and laughed.

I looked away from Mrs. Larson's piercing glare and down at my jeans. The tears fell down slowly because I didn't blink them away. I held my eyes open so the water wouldn't touch my eyelashes and disturb my mascara.

I heard the others move in their seats. "What is *wrong* with her?" someone whispered.

Mrs. Larson started to talk in more of a baby voice. "Oh no, honey, it's alright. You'll get it! You're just putting too much pressure on yourself."

I was always putting too much pressure on myself. It was always me who thought too much, and that was the problem. Then adults talked to me in a baby voice about it, which didn't help.

"It's okay, Paige. There's no need to cry."

It made me feel worse, like I was "overexaggerating" or "dramatic" or "too sensitive." I hated that our public classroom conversation turned from answering questions about the loss of innocence of Scout and Jem, to consoling Paige because she was crying loudly in the back of the class.

I didn't want to cry, just like no one else wanted me to cry. But there was nothing I could do with "There's no need to cry."

"Paige?" Mrs. Larson continued when I didn't respond. "Can you hear me?"

How embarrassing. How stupidly embarrassing it was to have my emotions as the center of attention in the first place. I felt like a child. I looked up at her because I couldn't handle the thought of her repeating herself.

I couldn't speak.

I just stared at her.

If I said something, I'd cry more.

My frustration was circular. There were no words left in my vocabulary to explain my meaning and my question. My mind was moving so fast with pictures and memories, none of which I could articulate, not even now as I think back. When my brain is acting like that, it can't focus on any one image. It can't hone in on a word or an answer.

With my brain overwhelmed in English class, it shut down my body, like it needed a manual restart.

"Paige, are you okay?"

I couldn't speak at all.

The bell rang after what seemed like forty-five years, the time spent mindless and vacant. I only shuddered and sniffled my way through. I remained seated. Still and silent. Tears fell onto my lap.

Sam stood at my desk for a while after the bell and waited for me to get up. I couldn't look at her. I didn't want to talk about it with her. Once every other student had left, Mrs. Larson told her to leave too. Sam hesitated, but I didn't protest, so she walked out, a little stiff. I could tell that I hurt her feelings, maybe even pissed her off. Another wave of tears.

Mrs. Larson locked the door behind Sam. She pulled up a chair beside my desk and leaned in front of me, trying to force eye contact. I began tidying my books to get ready to leave, to avoid whatever conversation my teacher wanted to have with me. She started talking before I could stand.

"I'll keep the door locked for ten minutes until the next class starts, and I'll have my kids from the next class wait outside until then. That means you're going to walk past them when you leave. Okay?"

I nodded. It was the best-case scenario we had at that point. I softened a little around my shoulders and sat deeper in my seat. I had ten minutes.

"Paige . . . This isn't normal."

Those were new words. They weren't said unkindly. They were factual and frank. They were a lifeline.

"What's going on?" she probed. "You cry almost every day. You can't handle getting anything wrong or not knowing the answer. You know what you're doing, you know how to write, but you don't trust yourself. This isn't good." She leaned farther forward in her chair. "Take a minute, breathe, do your thing, and maybe you should go to the guidance office. You can calm down there. Maybe they can help?"

Her words opened up an avenue I was willing to explore. No one had ever suggested that there might be someone who could help me. This had always been a *me* problem. And suddenly, maybe it wasn't. Or, if it was a me problem, there was someone who had ideas about what I could do with that.

The guidance office was pretty close to my English class, so I could potentially sneak there without too many people seeing me. I sat for the remaining nine minutes and stared at a doodle on my paper and focused on my surroundings and not my thoughts. Mrs. Larson made two phone calls: one to my next period class to let them know where I was, and one to the guidance office downstairs, to let them know about my arrival shortly and to make sure that got into the office's system so I wasn't marked absent. Weirdly, I felt . . . safe. After her phone calls, she walked back to her desk, sat down, and didn't look at me for the rest of the time.

It was kind of her. I noticed.

When it was time to walk out, I looked back at her to say goodbye. She only met my gaze and smiled without words, and I did the same. Mrs. Larson was officially one of my favorite teachers.

I walked downstairs to the guidance office and saw a really tall desk where the secretary usually sat. She wasn't there. I stood still and looked around to gather intel on my surroundings. A box sat on the table with a slit at the top for request slips for guidance sessions. Beside it were slips and a pen. Even though I couldn't speak, I could write on a slip. I wrote my name and slid it into the box.

A woman in her sixties, who was very tall and skinny with short dark hair and glasses, came into the space. She spoke kindly. "Can I help you?" she asked.

"Um . . . yeah," I said. My face turned red. I tried to form more words, but I began to cry again. "I wanna . . ."

She understood, it seemed. "Sit down, take a minute," she said and walked me from the reception area into a bigger room. It had four round tables and a huge window that took up almost one whole wall. It showed the main front street. The room smelled like Honey Nut Cheerios and pencil crayons. "You can have some snacks. Here are some coloring books. And if you want to come and talk to me, then you can do that." She left me at a table with a coloring book and some Cheerios and went back to her desk. Slowly, as time passed, I felt calmer.

I hung out in the guidance office, coloring and looking out the window, for the rest of the day. This was my first time in the guidance office. After that, it was a room I frequented for the rest of my high school experience. There were multiple guidance counselors who were also teachers of other subjects at the school. Students were assigned a counselor based on year, so all grade nines had the same guidance counselor. I only met with her twice, though. I met with at least six different people in the guidance office. Each tried to help me and offer advice and work with me on a schedule to keep me organized and not stressed out of my mind. They were nice and understanding in there. They gave me tissues and let me have a nap if I needed.

One really bad day, a guidance counselor was unable to console me and came up with a recommendation. She suggested I get my name on the list to see a for-real therapist who came to the school on Wednesdays. I eagerly accepted her recommendation and couldn't wait to meet with someone a little more specialized.

I texted my mom upon leaving the guidance office that day.

Me: i am not having a good time right now

Mom: Oh. I'm sorry to hear that.

Me: i went to the guidance office. they said i need some more help, which i agree with. they talked about some company across the street that they partner with, and apparently it's some kids' mental health program with therapists to help kids struggling with school-related anxiety

Mom: That sounds good!

A fire formed in my stomach. I was overwhelmed with frustration and sadness. Even though I was willing to try therapy, at that point, I was giving up on ever getting anyone to understand. My own mom didn't understand. How would anyone else? I was so deep in my pain that Mom's cheerful reply didn't seem like the answer of someone who really took my pain seriously. It was lighter to her than it was to me. I didn't know how to show her that I was trying so hard but never getting any better.

I reached out again for comfort.

Me: cause this really sucks.

Mom: I know, babe.

The therapist came from a child mental health service paid for by the school. Her name was Julie, she was very pregnant, and she had dozens of other students to see. Dozens of us, stressed enough that we were put on this roster. That made me feel like my problems were normal problems and that there were solutions. I was hopeful.

Julie told me that she read all my report cards and everything in my file and knew how stressed I was. I don't know what's in a file and who puts what in there. I imagined a teacher writing on a piece of paper to slide into the folder: "Paige was anxious today." I didn't get it.

"I just never have enough time," I whimpered to her during our first appointment. I squeezed my eyes shut, but the tears still fell. I could never stop them falling.

"What are all of the things you need to do? Let's make a list and make a schedule where everything gets done." Julie pulled out a pad of paper and pen. She was not bullshitting. She had no time for empathy, just results.

It was just what I needed. My brain ping-ponged thoughts everywhere, but now I could grab them and put them on the piece of paper. "Uh, homework for four classes, or three, really," I said. "Gym doesn't have homework. The homework should be separated and updated per week to include daily homework, assignments or project work, and studying for tests and exams."

"Okay."

"I dance on Tuesdays for two hours. But it takes fifteen minutes to drive there and back. It takes me about fifteen minutes to change and do my hair before we leave. So that's almost three hours now. And I need to shower every time I get home, because I am so gross after dance . . ." I snowballed, my brain speeding up again. I looked off into the distance and imagined my stressful Tuesdays. My nose began to run from crying so much.

"Right." She wrote. "Take your time, Paige."

"I don't like to eat right before dance, and I'm always hungry after, so eating is for after dance as well. After a shower. I take really long showers."

"How long?"

"Thirty to forty-five minutes."

"That is really long. Is that necessary?"

"No, but I can't take shorter ones right now. It's too hard to try that now, please?" I sobbed.

She passed me a tissue box.

"Please, is it okay if I take forty-five-minute showers?" I bent over and put my hands to my mouth to attempt to cover my wails.

We were having a perfectly normal conversation. She asked a perfectly normal question. *Gee, Paige, I notice you take excessively long showers, and if you are so stressed about time, why don't you take shorter showers?* A completely reasonable suggestion. But that's also why it sucked. Of course I knew I took unnecessarily long showers. There was no way to explain that forty-five minutes for a shower was necessary.

How could I explain?

Showers

- The transition from dry to wet. Body MUST be fully wet before hair is. If hair becomes wet, body IMMEDIATELY must become wet. I don't know why the feeling bothers me so much.
- The AWFUL transition from wet to dry, where it's cold and wet hair sends drops down your legs spontaneously.
- WET HAIR. Touching me. Touching my NECK. Getting stuck ON my neck like LEECHES.
- Hands in my hair while shampooing—hurt, heavy, uncomfortable, makes squeaky noises sometimes. I now use a silicone shampoo brush to help.
- Shaving is awful.

- WATER IN MY EYES. Water in my eyes as a kid was a huge
  fear of mine. During baths when I was little, Mom draped a
  facecloth over my eyes that I pressed hard onto so that no
  soap or water could seep through. It took a few minutes after
  my bath for my eyes to stop hurting and for my vision to
  return to normal. It was a very stressful time for me when I was
  little. It remained stressful every time I took a shower.
- SO LOUD.
- Showers take a long time because I can't do everything that
  needs doing quickly, even if I wanted to. If I did it quickly, I
  would not be doing it well. It is hell to all my senses.

My throat felt tight. I didn't want to talk about it anymore. I didn't
want to talk about showers.

"Paige, it's okay," Julie said. "We can look at that another time."

"Okay."

"So, I have the three classes of homework written down." She
wrote on a pale, yellow sticky note. "Then dance on Tuesdays," she
said. "What else do you do after school?"

"I get home at 3:30 p.m., also. That's probably important. We
usually have dinner as a family, but it's never the same time every
day because Mom and Dad work whenever and sometimes they
have appointments at dinnertime and sometimes we start at 5:00
but sometimes it's more like 6:30. How do you make a schedule
when there are things like that, circumstances out of your control?
How can you plan that?"

"I guess you can't."

"That's what bothers me, though."

"The unexpected? I know. Control what you can control. And
for now, that is going to be how you choose to spend your time. My
advice is that you don't diverge from this schedule as best as you can.
You'll have more confidence in a structure that doesn't fail you."

"How do we know it isn't going to fail me?"

"We don't."

I took the schedule with me to my next class. I pondered over it and worried how I could manipulate it when something came up or a plan changed. It wouldn't work otherwise. When I got home that night, Mom asked how the appointment went.

"Mom, I can't talk to you about it right now," I replied. I put my backpack down. "I need ten minutes to settle in and then I have twenty minutes of free space where I can explain."

She gave me space. Then I came back out into the kitchen and put the sticky note onto the counter. I talked her through when I was supposed to eat dinner and the general idea.

"That's good," Mom said. She frowned. "But what happens if your brother or your dad had to go to the hospital?"

"I don't know," I replied. My face got hot. "The therapist told me that there's no reason not to follow this schedule. What would my presence do to benefit the hospital situation? I wouldn't be necessary, and I'd be stressed about not doing my homework and my routine the whole time anyway."

"Right. But we need to be flexible, Paige," Mom said. "I don't want you to get stressed if you have to change this around."

Then I got really stressed because I knew there was nothing I could do about any of this. My face got hotter and I snapped, "Right, Mom, and I also don't want to be stressed if I have to change this. I cannot think about this right now or I will implode. I need to go to my room. I'm sorry. I love you." I marched into my room.

I tried to follow the sticky note for three days, but every day something upset the routine. The routine was unreliable and therefore useless, and I gave up. At the next appointment, Julie told me she was going on maternity leave. "Why don't you work on the routine with the next counselor?" she said. She touched her stomach lightly, maybe felt a kick. "They can help you figure out how to tweak this so it works for you."

"Great. Cool. Swag. Thanks. Uh, enjoy your baby."

The guidance office told me someone was going to replace Julie shortly. Until then, I belonged to the wolves, like the rest of the teenagers. If the school brought someone else in, I never met them. I wasn't put on that list.

> I realized it was a whole lot less stressful to just ignore those
> reading aloud and read the text in my own head myself.
>   I read the article before the teacher finished handing it out to
> the rest of the class behind me. Yet another activity that would be
> more efficient if I was alone.

School days passed, and I continued to dread dealing with altering my schedule when I got home. Even though the therapist was gone, and so was my path to getting help, I could at least try to figure that out. I tried to push down the dark thoughts that kept coming.

> I don't know how to live.
> This is too hard.
> I want to die.
> I want everything to stop.

I got started on my math homework thirty minutes after getting off the bus. That's what my schedule had suggested. I set my binder on the coffee table in the living room and worked away at algebraic problems. I thought I'd finish quickly, but the word problems slipped out from under me. My frustration grew as the hours went by and I still wasn't finished. I gritted my teeth and blinked my tears away.

Eventually my family returned home and dispersed to do their own things. Dad sat on the other couch and held the TV remote on his chest after he decided on a channel. I continued my work. The TV was distracting, but I could tune it out. I was tuning more and more out.

What was I missing all the time?

Why did I struggle so much?

Why did I have to get so upset about freaking grade nine math homework?

It got dark. I swallowed a cry and shuddered loudly. Dad turned down the TV. My stress filled the room like hot air. "Paige, why don't you go finish your homework in your room?" Dad said finally.

I broke down into a wave of tears. "What if I just stayed right here?"

"In the living room? The common area for the whole family?" Dad said.

Overwhelm

And then panic set in. My brain started to ping-pong unintelligible thoughts. Pictures and garbled jargon held a few slivers of phrases and images that were almost recognizable, but nothing coherent stuck together. My mind got louder, bolder, more intense, more pressurized. I couldn't explain my thoughts, or my feelings, or what I needed or wanted right then and there to let the pressure go. I just wanted to settle. I just wanted someone to take care of me. I just wanted to settle.

"I'm trying to relax after work," Dad said. "Take it somewhere else."

I didn't move. "I was here first," I said. "I didn't know there was a rule in this house saying no one is allowed to see you cry. I'm crying in front of you and you're like, *leave*? Thanks, Dad." I kept trying to do my math homework. Mom and Graham joined my dad to watch an episode of *Seinfeld*.

I continued to cry and freak out and panic, but I tried to do it all quietly. It was awkward and horrible. The canned laughter on the TV infiltrated my mind. Sometimes my family would laugh out loud. Eventually, I bundled my supplies inside the open page of my binder and carried everything into the kitchen. I didn't want to go into my room and have it seem like I let my father send me to my room for crying. I just wanted to finish my homework, not cry, and maybe have a little bit of family support.

In the kitchen, I looked at answers in the back of the textbook to help me. I looked through my notes and redid questions that I got right to confirm I knew how to do them. I googled, and watched YouTube explanations, and soon enough it was 10:30 p.m.

I didn't even get to my science or geography homework.

My parents said they wanted to go to bed and that I should do the same.

"I cannot go to bed. I'm not done with my homework. I'll go to bed when I'm done with my homework." They left the room and I sat, feeling abandoned, with the big light on, hopelessness and frustration in my heart.

I looked out of the window into the black sky. I wanted to see constellations and to stare at the moon and beg the stars to take my stress away. I wanted my brain to slow down. I dreamed of whatever could make it all stop, if only for a moment.

I could barely see outside beyond the reflection of the kitchen in the window. I got a gentle reminder of how ugly of a crier I was.

I could not do the homework.

I had to go to bed.

I tried to stand, but I was having a hard time breathing.

My legs didn't get enough oxygen, so it was hard to operate any muscles to walk. I slumped back against the wall with my rag-doll legs tingling in front of me. Every part of my body craved oxygen, but the fight only made it worse. I couldn't stop crying. I left my body and it shook and cried and rolled around on the floor without me.

When the brain doesn't get enough oxygen, it sends a message to the body to get on the ground so that gravity can assist in getting adequate blood supply, and therefore oxygen, to the brain. I felt so powerless when I was forced to succumb to the will of my body; no matter how badly I wished to remain alert and strong, my vision went dark and my head went limp. It was a few seconds or a few minutes.

When I woke up, I realized the left side of my head hurt, and I wasn't crying and hyperventilating anymore. I stood up and looked at the clock:

12:17 A.M.

Without even brushing my teeth, I went straight to bed.

It bothered me when a teacher couldn't explain a concept to a struggling student. Often, I knew how to explain it so that it would click for my classmate. Knowing how to answer better than the teacher filled the inside of me with pressure, a pressure I had to contain, build, and release very, very slowly. I worked very hard at containing that pressure. I was a good teacher. This is not me being cocky; this is me sharing a fact. I had a way of explaining things that made sense to people. A concept, a movement, a word, a dance, a pattern. I knew how to listen to someone's question and find out what it was they didn't understand and explain it to them in exactly the right way. It took years of training for me to hold all of the pressure in and let the teacher continue explaining poorly. But when I was still in grade nine, the pressure went all the way to my hand and raised it up high in the air to lecture the class "politely" with an explanation. Math was my best subject.

My grade nine math teacher was frustrating for most of us. I felt like, deep down, she knew her stuff and she knew what she was talking about, but her words just came out so wrong that they confused everybody. She got flustered when too many people had questions, sent kids to the office willy-nilly, and repeated what she'd previously said, only louder, thinking that made a difference.

Math is just a bunch of patterns. My hand went up so I could explain that pattern. I wanted to help other kids understand just as easily as I did.

Due to assigned seating, Sam and I didn't sit together in math. I sat at the very front of the class, which was something I told my teachers I preferred when they did seating changes.

Sam was close by—one column to the right of me and a few rows behind. She was okay being in the middle. She was okay anywhere.

One May afternoon, in the last twenty minutes of a grade nine math class, Sam had a question. I put down my doodling to turn around and look at her. Usually, I tuned out the class after I finished the work, but it was her voice that drew my attention. Sam asked questions when she needed to, and she knew how to word her question to say exactly what she meant. She never misspoke.

I didn't hear her question, so I didn't want to listen to the teacher's answer (because then I would get frustrated and need to ask what Sam's question was in order for me to understand where we were in the conversation). I watched my friend's curious face, waiting for it to shift into understanding and glance back down at her paper as the teacher explained.

It did not.

After the teacher responded, Sam tilted her head more to the side and brought her eyebrows closer together. Two other students said, "What?" as they tried to figure it out too.

I faced the board to see the teacher staring back at Sam, like if she stared long enough into her eyes, the knowledge would transfer from one brain to the other.

Game time for Paige.

I saw the question on the board and solved it, now prepared to listen to Sam's rebuttal.

"Huh. Okay. I didn't see it like that at first," Sam said. I could tell that was fluff. She was just being nice. "I think I'm stuck on looking at x, and how the sign changes in the next step," she added.

Ahhhh! Just say "division." She'll get it if you just say "division."

I waited for the teacher to say the magic words. The. Words. Did. Not. Come.

Instead, the teacher spoke in circles and made awful connections that made even those of us who understood the material confused. A shiver went down my back, and I cringed. The pressure started to build. I spoke softly over to Sam to help.

"Sam, *how* does x move to the other side?" I asked her, rhetorically.

Division. She knew the answer. Then she would understand. But she wasn't looking at me. She kept looking at the teacher, intently listening with her eyes. She didn't hear me, I guess.

"Sam," I whispered again.

Our teacher kept talking, and I listened to hear if it was still garbage. It was.

"Sam, I can help you," I whispered again.

She still wasn't looking at me. She heard me. People behind her looked over to see me speak, so I know she heard me. When people don't look at you at all, it's because they're trying not to.

I turned back around to face my desk as my face went hot and tears bubbled up behind my eyes. I purposely didn't listen to the teacher because it only would have aggravated me more, so I listened to my thoughts instead and counted the seconds that passed until the conversation was over.

Sam still didn't get it.

I knew Sam. She was a smart girl. Her brain didn't find patterns as quickly as mine did, but it was still very good at holding onto them. If someone had explained it right, she would have understood.

Work continued for the remaining fifteen minutes until the bell rang. Finally, I moved.

I stood up and walked over to Sam's desk casually. She gathered her books and strutted into the hallway, not even acknowledging my much slower pace.

"Dude, wait!" I said to her.

She slowed down and turned to face me but didn't look in my eyes. She didn't stop walking and kept her pace in front of me instead of beside.

That was not her normal behavior.

"What's wrong?" I asked. I was supposed to ask.

"I was trying to listen," she snapped.

I thought that's what this was about. I didn't even miss a beat. "Why? She doesn't know what she's talking about."

"Yeah, she does, Paige."

Oh?

That threw me back, as the saying goes, but also because it made me stop in my tracks while Sam kept walking with her long strides.

"I didn't know you thought that," I said.

Sam noticed my faraway voice and turned back around to talk to me. We were outside the bathrooms, the noise of the school around us. We moved over to the side of the hall so as not to block traffic. We were both very calm, despite being upset.

"I thought it was universal—that we all knew that she didn't know what she's talking about," I said. "I'm sorry."

"You do it all the time, Paige." Sam still wasn't looking at me.

"What?"

"You try to explain something while the teacher is also explaining it."

"Do I?" I hadn't noticed.

"Yes, and it's hard to listen to either of you."

"Dude, I had no idea I even did that . . . Why didn't you tell me?"

She bit her lower lip.

"I could've changed that if you just said something sooner."

"I shouldn't *have* to say something," Sam said. She was almost angry.

"Sam?! How can you expect me to read your mind? That isn't fair," I replied, shocked that we were having this conversation, that this was happening in the hallway by the bathrooms.

"I can't do anything to fix it if you don't tell me," I said.

"Okay! Fine! Whatever," she replied. She turned to face the direction of her locker and walked away.

I didn't follow. I didn't move. I stood by the bathrooms for a few minutes, unmoving in the bustling hallway. I stared at the ground and I didn't know what to do next.

Do I follow her?

It's too late now, she's probably gone from her locker by this time. Good job, Paige.

I can't stand here alone weirdly in the hallway. I look like a zombie.

Who cares what other people think?

Me. I do. I care what Sam thinks.

What the heck was that?!

I guess that's something that I do.

But I always explain things better! I don't see how it's a problem!

But now I understand!

Do I tell Sam this?

In person? Text her? Call her?

After a few minutes of my best statue impersonation, I reluctantly took steps forward, which led to more and more until I took 128 steps and faced my locker. I gathered my stuff. I walked outside to catch my bus, and I didn't see Sam along the way.

And then it was awkward at dance that night, because I didn't know what to say and neither did she. So, we just didn't talk.

And then we didn't talk the next day in class.

We didn't talk at dance that night either.

Then a week went by and we still didn't talk.

Two weeks.

Three.

Panic attacks could be scary to navigate alone. They made me feel like I was going to die. I had more and more panic attacks as high school continued. I searched my symptoms online to try to figure out what was going on with me. Even though I got the words "panic attack" from the internet, I still didn't know *why* I always ended up there. I knew I was stressed, but I couldn't work out why it was so much, so intense, all the time.

I battled my thoughts in the car driving home and in bed while falling asleep. I struggled daily with school. Because I couldn't take in enough oxygen when I had a panic attack, these episodes sometimes ended with me passing out. If that happened at school, I slumped on my desk. When it happened at home, I tried to stay in my room.

Mom didn't know what to do for me when I had them, and I didn't know either. I still didn't have a therapist at school. Mom and I tried a couple of times to find help and resources from our family doctor, Dr. Hallix, but we'd gotten nowhere. I really didn't like my doctor because he *really* didn't like it when I asked him questions. He didn't do anything substantial. It was like he didn't really see a problem. He didn't want to diagnose me with anything, he wouldn't prescribe me with any medication, and he didn't believe things were that hard. "It's perfectly normal to be stressed, and you need to learn to manage it," he said.

You're making it up, Paige. You're being manipulative. You're trying to get attention.

Grade nine ended. It was summer.

I wanted to die.

Interlude

It wasn't all dark. I kept myself busy.

Prepping for dance competitions, working every day.

Theater in my free time.

And Max.

Max was around, more and more.

There wasn't a person alive who understood me like Max Miller. The inner workings of our brains were almost similar; not like how family members were similar, but like how neighbors were similar. He saw my perspective almost exactly, even though he got to that perspective differently.

All the times I cried alone in my room, I felt comfort knowing I was able to reach out to Max. He was so busy after school with all his sporting activities, but he made even the smallest amount of time for me every day. He called me while in the locker room before a big hockey game for a few minutes to say he was going to score a goal for me. He sent me messages late at night when he got home while I slept, and I woke up to them in the morning with a big smile on my face. He let me rant to him about my feelings and helped me sort them out when he was available. It wasn't one-sided; I did the same for him. I wanted to. I was so thankful.

That summer, I spent as many days as I could with Max. His facade dropped, but only as much as he could allow, so still he flirted and teased and tried stupid pickup lines.

"You've got me. You know that, right?" I asked him. We sat at a park bench by the water eating ice cream.

"Yeah, and you've got me," he replied, ice cream dripping down his knuckles.

I picked up a small spoonful. "No, like, you've got me. You don't have to try and impress me, or audition for me, or convince me to hang out with you. I like you for who you are today, and the actions you take that show me who that person is."

"You're funny," he said. "This whole time I thought you were becoming more like you. Really, I'm becoming more like me too."

"Yeah . . . I'm really happy for us."

"I'm really happy." He squeezed my hand with his clean hand, and he kissed me. "What if someone asked me what we were . . . Can I start saying you're my girlfriend?"

I got butterflies in my stomach in a way that made me want to jump up and down and wave my hands and squeal. So, I did, because I did around Max. And I said, "I think you might have been my boyfriend before, anyways, so this is perfect!" And I gave him a big hug and got his ice cream in my hair. I knew I would have to pull my hair into a ponytail so the wet ice cream didn't touch my shoulder, and I would have to shower when I got home, but I swatted those ping-pong thoughts away with Max's clean hand.

Mom and I agreed that although she didn't know how to help me, she could definitely offer a hug when I had a panic attack. Frequently I emerged from my bedroom to hunt for my mother to ask her for a really tight, soul-crushing hug. Sometimes I asked if she could sit with me and talk.

One evening, after trying to calm myself down in my room and failing, I found Mom putting laundry away in her room. She stood next to her closet with her clothes on the bed, putting them away one by one. I joined the clothes on the bed and talked and cried about my stressful science test and my stressful life.

Mom said it was normal. "I know. I know you don't like to hear it, but I think it's true, babe. Your feelings are normal. All of this is normal." She pleaded with me to see her point of view, to see myself as normal and okay.

But I refused. "*No!* Mom, listen to me!" I didn't mean to yell, but I did. I was heaving, not breathing. My sobs increased. I sounded like a zombie. *Aaaaarrrhhh*. I yelled by accident. "How can you say this is normal when it's so bad?" I couldn't hold in my tears, and I started gasping in sync with my sobs. The air was harsh, scraping through my throat. There was just so much to swallow. My lungs were so hungry. My hands flapped up and down.

Mom stopped folding laundry, sat on the bed, and looked at me. "Because, Paige, everyone gets worked up and stressed about the things they're passionate about." She reached across to put her hand on my thigh, forgetting that I hated it. I tried to tolerate her touch, then moved her hand off my leg. She added, "People may not show it like you do, but everyone's having a hard time. Everyone feels this way."

"I wish you understood how painful that is to hear from you."

Silence. She didn't have a response. While she waited for mine, she started to cry.

"If everyone felt this way," I continued, "a lot of people would kill themselves because this is horrible. This isn't how anyone should live life."

Mom was pretty fluent in understanding me through tears. "You work yourself up, sweetheart." It really did bother her to see me in pain, and I know she was trying to calm me. "You don't have to worry so much. You're going to be alright."

"When?"

"I don't know, but someday!"

"What if someday is too far away and I can't make it that long? Mom, I can't do this for long. There's always eighteen thousand things to do and that's so many things and I don't have enough time. And then when I do have time on the weekends, I work, and I don't know why, before work I sit and I *can't do anything for hours*."

I gave up with my makeup and let it run down my slobbery face. "I swear this isn't an 'everyone' thing. Look at me. I cry all the time. I am so stressed."

"That's because you're a good student," Mom tried again to interrupt my snowball. "And you're kind and you're sensitive and you pour your heart and soul into every single thing you do. You work very hard and you're very ambitious . . ."

"I don't want to be ambitious, Mom . . ." I slumped over on the bed. "I want to be stupid."

"Well, I don't know if we can make that happen for ya." She giggled. It bothered me when she tried to joke at times like this. She had to when she was uncomfortable, but it made me feel worse.

I rocked back and forth on the bed.

This conversation fizzled out, as it always did, with nary a solution or a plan in place. We reached the same conclusion every time; neither one of us knew what to do to help me. I probably wasn't going to get any help at this point, at this time, and we had nowhere else to go. Eventually, we had to leave her room and move on with our lives. Except I didn't want to move on. I wanted to give up. I could not keep doing this anymore.

This time, Mom surprised me.

"Okay. You know what we're going to do?" Mom said. "We're going to book an appointment with Dr. Hallix. We're gonna figure this out. 'Cause you're right. This isn't okay. It's not fair."

I nodded but didn't feel any better. Dr. Hallix had never helped before.

"If it's medication you need, then maybe that's what we do. Or maybe he can find a therapist or someone for you to talk to. We'll make him offer something this time."

Yes. I nodded.

She reached for a hug, and I accepted. I put my arms over hers and we both squeezed each other tightly and tried not to snot in each other's hair.

FIELD NOTES

I couldn't believe I got Mom to understand.

I couldn't believe Dr. Hallix was actually going to do something.

I just turned fifteen.

Dr. Hallix referred me for an appointment with a child psychiatrist.

Life was going to be okay.

CHAPTER 9

THE END OF THE BEGINNING

light in the dark

a diagnosis,
or a label,
a name, a category, a group . . .
is relieving
because it says
somebody understands you.

not like
that black hole
of internal isolation
when you feel
complete individualization.

there is comfort
in shared struggle.

I'LL NEVER FORGET THE PSYCHIATRIST'S SUDDEN CHANGE OF expression. "Alright, Paige. You've done everything you need. Now it's my turn."

Ahh. *That's* what he was like when we started. Nice. Kind. Definitely good with kids. I was taken aback by his sweet demeanor.

He kept his cool while making me lose mine. I was manipulated. Outsmarted. He knew what to do to get a reaction out of me, and I was left all worked up while he snapped back to emotional regularity. It was mad impressive. I didn't know people could switch their emotions so easily, so quickly, and control them to that extent. I was irritating and annoying and asked too many questions, and usually that made people frustrated with me. It turns out, you can pretend to feel one way when you actually feel another.

I don't think the psychiatrist was ever actually irritated by me. I don't think he was affected emotionally at all. He just had to be serious and diligent and provide the best assessment possible. I wasn't sure if that made me feel better or worse, to know that he wasn't mad at me. It was good to feel like I hadn't done anything wrong, but I still didn't have the most fun thinking he was yelling at me.

Once I noticed what he did, I looked away, my mouth dropping open in shock. I giggled a little and stopped crying. I'd been bested, and I didn't even see it coming. I respected him for that. I was confident that this man could tell me something helpful, if he was able to penetrate my brain like that to extract information.

I turned to face Mom, and she was already facing me. She had tears in her eyes. She grabbed my hand and squeezed, looking back up at the analyst, whose name was Dr. Turner. I squeezed her hand back. It meant, *Here it is. The moment we've been waiting for.*

But before he began to speak, I released Mom's hand and she retreated hers back to her lap. I was a sweaty mess. I did not wish to *touch.* I touched my other hand, the hand Mom didn't grab, to transfer some of the *touch* so my hands felt even.

I did not wish to look. I gazed at the floor and let my vision blur out of focus.

"Wow, Paige. First of all, before I start this next part with you, I just wanted to say thank you for sharing everything that you did today. I know this process is not an easy one, and it can be scary to allow someone into the deepest parts of your mind. Thank you for being so open. It really allows me to get to know you better and get you the proper treatment."

Gee, thanks. It *was* hard. I was glad he recognized that. But it was the kind of hard I chose, because it was better than the hard I already had.

I didn't know what to say back to him. *You're welcome? No problem?* I said nothing. Without looking up, I nodded and flashed a grin as a positive visual response.

"What you struggle with is real. It's so apparent and prevalent in your everyday life, and I can't believe no one brought anything to your mother's attention, or got you help or a therapist or . . . even just some time to chill out. And I'm really sorry that happened to you. Your schools never had psychologists?"

"Nope," Mom responded.

"Really? Well, I'm really glad we got to talk now. It's about time someone gives you some answers. How are you feeling now, Paige? Tired?"

"Yeah," I said. "I'm sorry, that was just a lot."

"No, that's okay." I felt like it was okay. I could almost take a breath.

"So, you came in here struggling with a lot of stress and anxiety with just about everything: school and your other activities, the uncontrollable urges and feelings and thoughts you have, feeling numb and empty and like you can't make a right move in any direction. You were kind of thinking maybe 'anxiety,' maybe 'depression,' and, yep, I'd say so too, definitely. That's pretty clear. But that's not all, and that's not even the root cause of what's going on, why you feel so worked up. They're just side effects, really, of the main issue here . . . And that is that you are autistic."

Autistic?

He described the criteria in the DSM-5. Everything he said chipped away something hard inside of me. I felt lighter and lighter with each sentence. The last fifteen years of my life were explained on a random Tuesday. So simply.

"It's called autism spectrum disorder," he continued. "Basically, your brain formed differently than everyone else's brain. It reacts differently to stimuli, usually more intensely—like how you can't wear dresses in the winter with snow pants, and cut the tags out of your clothes, and didn't let your mom brush your hair. It's different than a mental illness. It's actually not an illness at all, but it can be very hard being autistic. We're able to treat some of the unpleasant co-occurring symptoms, like depression and anxiety and OCD."

I stared at the floor. I don't really remember what he said next. It was like everything in my life started capsizing. His words changed the perspective of my whole entire life.

The one thing I kept thinking over and over was: *I'm not crazy. I'm not making it up. I'm not manipulative or trying to fake anything. I am actually really not having an okay time and I haven't been for a while, and there's a reason why. There's a reason why I'm the way that I am. There's a reason why I feel the things I feel and do the things I do. And it's not because I am an attention seeker or a drama queen or a diva. So many of my questions have one clear answer. Every part of me is autistic. I've been autistic for fifteen years and this psychiatrist is just figuring it out now.*

"Depression? I'm depressed?" I finally surfaced enough to ask.

"Well, yes, Paige. People who want to kill themselves are usually depressed."

"But I don't want to kill myself because I'm sad or empty, but because my brain goes so fast, and I want things to stop."

"That makes sense. Have you ever seen *The Big Bang Theory*, Paige?"

"That is my favorite show, actually."

"Are you going to mention Sheldon Cooper next, doctor?" Mom asked.

"Yes, I am."

"That's funny, because we always compare Paige to Sheldon Cooper."

"Paige," the doctor said, "you're like Sheldon Cooper but smarter."

I scoffed a little bit, because Sheldon Cooper was a physicist. And I was just fifteen and didn't know anything, really, about physics or anything else.

"You're smarter than Sheldon Cooper," he continued, "because you've learned so much about humans. You tricked everyone around you for years, as safely as possible. Tell me, have you ever thought that everyone else seemed to be able to speak to each other in ways that you couldn't understand or be involved in? Did you feel they understood a lot of what you didn't, without explanation? Almost like you missed a lesson in class or something before being born about how to be human?"

I stared at the floor, trying to process.

"It must've been so exhausting for you," he continued. "You've spent your whole life observing other people and judging yourself and trying to create a persona that will be accepted in society. That's why people know Sheldon Cooper is autistic but didn't know that you were. Because you've developed a trick that will camouflage you, so you blend in as much as possible with everyone else. That's called masking."

My face was so disgustingly wet with tears. "Are you sure I'm not a narcissist?" I asked, a word that worried me.

"You're definitely not a narcissist, Paige." He smiled like I'd asked a silly question. "The fact that you're coming here *concerned that you are* is pretty much proof enough of that."

I *wasn't* manipulative?

"You memorized movies and television show scripts word for word, just from watching them. How old were you, you said, when you did that Barbie movie recital for your parents?"

Barbie and the Magic of Pegasus was released shortly after my fifth birthday.

"And when did you start acting?"

"Six."

"Why did you take to acting so quickly? Could it be because you were already acting like a pro every day? Acting is like what you do all the time, except someone else helps you decide where to move and when, what to say, how to say it, who to say it to . . . The script is already written. You know exactly what the next person is going to say. You know how every argument is going to end. In that situation, you're in control. You can prepare yourself. You know what facial expressions you're going to use, how you're going to move your body. You practiced them dozens of times and received confirmation that you did look like a normal person. That is, of course, part of what makes a great actor: the ability to convince the audience in that time and space that they're not acting. And you're a great actor, aren't you, Paige?"

"The greatest," Mom replied. She looked sad for a moment, gazing at something I couldn't see.

He continued to explain every part of my life and why it never made sense. Mom and I tried to sit like sponges, but my sponge was fully saturated.

"I notice you like to touch something with both of your hands. The chair you're sitting on, for example. Or when your mum grabs one of your hands, you let go and then have to touch your other hand." Dr. Turner continued to describe traits he noticed about me during our session.

"You feel a need for symmetry. How much does that bother you in dance?"

"Oh my gosh," I responded. "*So much*. If we turn on our right foot at all, I need to turn the same number of times on my left foot, regardless of whether the teacher asks us to."

"What if someone said to you, 'Paige, whatever you do, *don't* go outside tomorrow or the world's going to end in a flaming asteroid ball of fire!' What would you do?"

"What?! I'd stay inside."

"Really?"

"Yes."

"You'd listen to a random stranger on the street, and trust them over the trust that you have that the world isn't going to end tomorrow?"

"Why would you go outside and risk flaming balls of space death rock falling to Earth?! I don't want that. I was probably just going to stay inside most of the day anyway, so it's not like it's a big deal."

"Don't you want to die, though?"

Wow. It was so different from that. "I may want to die but preferably not by being hit with an asteroid and succumbing to whatever injuries that gives me . . ."

"Okay, you're right, Paige . . ." He tried to cut me off, but I didn't allow it.

"Plus, I don't want to kill my whole family and every person I love—"

"True, okay," he interrupted. I continued to speak over him.

"And all babies on the Earth, and animals, and innocent things that don't deserve that? No way, man." I imagined asteroids hitting a forest of baby deer and bears and frogs and birds, and tears filled my eyes. I slumped back to cry and listen.

"That makes sense, Paige. I don't mean to question your morality. But I am curious why you would stay home, because most people would actually probably not listen. Most people would still go outside the next day, even if someone said it would end the world."

"What?! Why? How does that make sense? That's literally the plot of every teen movie ever. The parents or the city or the religion says, 'Don't do this thing,' and then the characters don't listen and do the thing they aren't supposed to, the bad consequences that they knew would happen, happen, and they have to try and get out of it."

"Most people don't do that. They think, 'Wow, that's a crazy person. The world's totally not going to end in asteroid rain if I step outside tomorrow.'"

"But how do you know that? What if they know something you don't?"

"You don't trust yourself at all. You threw away a fact of your life that you know to be true, and that is that you definitely do not control asteroids."

It seemed he was trying to make clear that following my compulsions wasn't helping me. That my compulsions weren't my reality.

"So, what do we do?" Mom said. "What are our next steps?"

I was frustrated, scared, and worn out. My exhausted brain tried to gather pieces of information he shared with us, but the pieces were getting lost after all these hours sitting in those chairs.

"So, there isn't enough known about autism," he said, "particularly autism in girls, as it usually presents differently than boys, considering how they're socialized. Your best bet is to find someone trained in autism, no matter what you go to therapy for, because every single thing that makes you anxious or depressed is built differently and that is what needs to be understood.

"There's nothing wrong with being autistic," he continued. "There's nothing that you, Mom, have done wrong or did to cause this. You may hear stories about autism being caused by vaccines or autism being treated or cured with magic pills and potions, but there is zero scientific evidence to suggest those absurd claims and an abundance of evidence against them. There is a heavy genetic component, though. That means that it is likely that someone in your family is autistic, and also your kids are more likely to be autistic, Paige. To your knowledge, no one in the family is autistic? Or has ADHD, which you could have as well?"

"None diagnosed that I know of, but your dad's probably autistic," Mom said.

"Really?!" I said, astonished. This day was full of revelations.

"Oh yeah, all of the problems you're describing, how you feel all the time, your dad's the same," Mom said. Her words were so casual.

I didn't know what to make of that, but I didn't know what to make of any of the appointment so far. I was stunned. Why hadn't anyone made any of these connections, then? Why did Dad turn away from my anguish? He was never there to console me. He never seemed to believe me, even.

"You won't find many older people diagnosed with autism," the psychiatrist said. "Some people wonder, 'Why are more and more people getting diagnosed with autism today? What's going on to create more autistic people now as opposed to fifty years ago?' And the answer is, we're finding those autistic people, we're helping those autistic people, we're not throwing them in straightjackets and padded rooms and stuffing them with pills and labeling them 'crazy.' And a lot of them were like you, Paige, and struggled in silence. They learned to mask, like you did. They kept it up inside, behind closed doors, behind their job, behind anything they could focus on and control or escape. A lot of autistic adults struggle with substance abuse as a way to cope with their difficult reality."

"Holy crap. I couldn't imagine living that long without knowing," I said.

"Neither can a lot of autistic people," he replied.

The entire session took about three hours. I left with three diagnoses: generalized anxiety disorder, depression, and autism spectrum disorder.

Dr. Turner faxed a diagnosis to Dr. Hallix. I assumed next steps would be presented. A path, finally, but we never heard from Dr. Turner again. While I'm grateful that he shed the light that he did, I still had a long journey to travel. We said our thank-yous and goodbyes, the monitor blinked off, and Mom and I left the room.

CHAPTER 10

AFTERMATH

new rules

you're allowed to grow and change.
you're allowed to be wrong,
learn from it,
and live differently.
i hope you do.

THE HOSPITAL WING WAS NEARLY VACANT. I WATCHED MY FEET reach the elevator. We were wrapped in silence until we got out of the hospital and the rush of hot, humid air knocked the first words out of Mom.

"Whew! That's a lot, eh?" she said.

I nodded. It was a lot.

"That's a lot, eh, Paige?" she echoed, seeking my response.

"Yes, that's a lot."

In the truck, she said, "Man, I wish I had that on film."

"Me too." I already felt the important things he said slipping away. My brain was still numb. Soon we'd be home, and I could close the door behind me and process.

We did drive-through McDonald's before heading home.

The boys weren't home yet; Dad was working and Graham was at a friend's. They both knew I was going to the psychiatrist that day and would catch up with any news later. The house was quiet and warm with summer. I went to my room and took a nap.

That day, in the aftermath, I woke to my family chattering in the kitchen and checked my phone: 6:28 p.m. Dinnertime.

I continued to lie on my bed. I scrolled through Ask.fm, an old social media app where you could ask questions anonymously. I didn't ask anyone questions; instead I answered questions for other people: stupid questions, questions about my thoughts on life, questions about periods, questions about being a teenager. Nothing about autism. The murmur of the distant kitchen conversation, the babble of their voices, the rhythm of our lives together, was background.

Eventually I joined them, because Dad made steak. He'd pulled out the steaks that morning because I loved them, and we had food I liked for dinner on days when I would need a pick-me-up. I guess he knew I was going to have a "steak for dinner" kind of day with the psychiatrist.

> Dad made me uncomfortable when he ate. No matter what was presented to Dad on his plate, he stirred it all up and created a sloppy pile of mush. He ate everything all together, with each bite containing a little bit of each item on the plate. The meat juices bled into the rice, tainting the original flavor. Peas broken and smashed into shreds of meat and sauces and potatoes (and there were always so many potatoes), and potatoes are not good to me. I don't like their mushy texture and their bland taste.

I didn't look at any of them but could feel all of their heads angled toward me. I was hungry, so I grabbed my empty plate and walked to the counter to serve myself. I don't like my food to intermingle. I placed steak, potatoes, peas, and HP sauce separately, neatly. None of them touching each other. I took my seat again. Everyone was quiet. I had given Mom permission to tell the boys what happened at my appointment while I napped, so I assumed that now they knew.

Mom and Dad started a typical conversation about a couple who lived nearby and a new job that someone had. It was chatter to me. I focused on trying to eat. In this space, my thoughts were that I had no idea what to say, what to do, what to think. All I could do was try to eat. There were times that I caught Graham looking at me, trying to see if I was doing okay. Mom chimed in with, "Do you want anything to drink?"

"No," I replied.

"Milk? Water? Gatorade? Juice?"

"No, thanks."

Dad took a piece of cut steak, slid it off his fork and onto my plate. It was a generous gift, considering I loved steak very much, and he did as well.

I wanted to enjoy the gift. I wanted to be thankful and happy. I felt guilty that I wasn't—that I felt differently than I was supposed to. But I was frustrated that I could not enjoy a lovely piece of steak because it also had peas and potato and HP sauce on it.

"Are you sure you don't want me to get you a drink, Paige?" Mom asked.

"If I wanted a drink, I would have gotten one. Thank you."

Then they all exchanged looks that meant, *Whoa, don't talk to Paige right now.* And no one talked to me again for the rest of the night. I put my dirty dishes away and was excused from the table. I went to sleep.

I planned to go into town the next day to see Max. Mom drove me from our house and dropped me off at the mall. Max arrived just before I did and had already gotten drinks for both of us. We wandered around the mall and around town, making our way to his house.

"So, how did the appointment go?" he asked, looking at me seriously. I still hadn't shared it with him, not wanting to tell him over the phone or by text.

"Can we wait until we get to your house?" I asked. "I don't—"

"Of course."

We walked south on the sidewalk, without ever having to turn in any other direction. We held hands.

"When people hold hands but not tightly, it's like they don't even want to hold hands," I said.

His right hand gripped mine tightly. His thumb was in front of mine with our fingers interlocking. "This is the proper way to hold hands," he said. "Like you want to."

"Right? Even when it gets sweaty."

"It's lazy to do it any other way. None of that loose finger crap."

"Nonchalant."

"Complacent." He grabbed me and moved me to his left, so he was on the edge of the sidewalk.

"What's that about?"

"No one's going to see you when they're driving, because you're so short. I'll stand next to the cars. I want to protect you from getting hit by a car. Got it, babe?" He grinned at me and lightly pinched the back of my arm. That was him being flirty. I loved it. Everything about him just made me melt. That and the hot day. And the upcoming conversation.

Got it, babe.

Max was truly my best friend too. It surprised me how well he took my problems.

It was also incredible to share so much of myself with another person. He cared so much. He remembered every single thing that

I said to him. He knew if and when I got overwhelmed, a lot of times before it even happened, and he would get me out of that situation. He briefed me before any new location or new scenario or new person. He gave me sentences to say or questions to ask others. He reminded me to eat and wear a jacket. He knew what things I didn't understand, and he helped me and accommodated me with every single one of them. It was a marvelous connection that felt like love.

We arrived at his house and went into his kitchen to grab some water.

"Okay, so . . . You met Dr. Temple Run or whoever." He grabbed me by the waist and lifted me up, placing me on the counter in front of him. He looked me in the eyes and leaned forward, showing that he was paying a lot of attention and really listening. "Tell me all about it. Everything okay?"

"Oh yeah, I'm not dying or anything. I'm still pretty shocked about it, though. I don't even really know what it means . . ."

"What? Did they diagnose you with something?"

"Yeah, with a few things, actually."

"Okay. So, anxiety, depression, right?" He knew me so well.

"Yes, but apparently it's because of something else even bigger . . ." My mouth was dry. "I'm autistic."

He didn't change his expression or look away. "Okay. What's that mean?"

I explained all my problems that were themselves explained by autism.

"Makes sense, baby girl." His voice was relaxed, calm. He went to the fridge and got out orange juice for me.

"But I'm still me!" I made sure to note this. I couldn't tell how he felt, and so I reassured him, asked him, begged him in these words to think of me as the same, regardless. "I haven't changed at all. The diagnosis is all about finding out something about yourself, not creating something about yourself." I stared at his kitchen floor.

"I'm glad you're going to be able to get some help," he said. He poured juice into a glass for me. "Maybe, though, you shouldn't tell people for a while?"

He passed me my juice.

"Not tell anyone?" I sipped, now making eye contact with him.

"Not until you figure it out and understand what it means to you." He poured himself a water.

"Oh, I guess." I drank from my juice. It was cool and sweet. I was fifteen.

how did his brain
know so much about mine and yet was so different?
and on the same path

in order to survive, although we were different,
we both had to know
what other people were thinking and feeling all the time

to both of us
his words were his way of saying,
they're not ready to know about that, yet.

"Besides, I like being the only one who knows," he said, chugging his water and smiling over at me.

I left Max at his house and Mom picked me up. We drove home in silence, watching our small town become fields, the sun falling through the sky.

"Dad and I talked last night," Mom told me.

"What did he say? Does he think the diagnosis is wrong?" My chest was on fire. I was anxiously awaiting to hear Dad's verdict, one that he shared only with Mom but passed down through the house.

"No," Mom replied. "He said, 'Maybe *I'm* autistic.'"

I knew what Mom had said the day before, but this still surprised me. "No way . . ."

"Way."

My dad was the kind of guy who didn't let me take Advil if I had a headache. I went to school unless I was "broken or bleeding," and he always said, "You're fine."

But I wasn't fine. I hadn't been fine for a long time. And now he was saying that he wasn't fine either. It made me curious. I never thought that we were similar. I realized I really didn't know my dad.

When I went to bed that night, I didn't sleep well.

FIELD NOTES

- I was scared. I was already the weird kid who cried all the time and was so stressed that she wanted to die every single day, and that was just neutral public knowledge.
- I so badly wanted to call Sam and say, "Sam, I'm sorry. I didn't mean to be bossy and push you away from me. I'm autistic. I swear I never meant to hurt you, and if you tell me what hurts I will attend to it. Please, can we be friends again?" But those three weeks of not speaking became four weeks and then became months and I didn't pick up the phone.
- What was autism anyway?
- What did anybody at my school or in my town know about autism?
- Wanna know how many times I heard the word "autism" growing up? Probably two, in my whole life.
- One time I heard about a guy in my year who had a younger brother with Asperger's. He talked about it.
- One other time on a TV show.
- It was great to have a name for me. Life truly restarted. Now I knew I was different. I *knew* I was different. I wasn't faking it. I wasn't fine.

When Mom vacuumed at home, I went to my room and shut the door. The vacuum was so loud; it bothered my ears and my mind. I couldn't think when there was a loud noise. I noticed my friends weren't bothered by the same things. In fact, some of them even enjoyed loud noise, or said they didn't even notice it.

Then, when Mom knocked on my bedroom door twice and entered before I could say anything, my brain went numb. I froze to try to look normal as Mom came into my room to vacuum. I didn't want her to think I was acting strangely. I barely had the ability to nod at her. Sometimes all I could do was smile and blink at the same time. She knew that this meant I wanted her to leave me alone and get out of my room quicker.

Oftentimes, my eyes stopped moving during a blast of loud noise. They got stuck wherever they looked right before it happened and were incapable of moving, because moving my eyes required thinking as to where I wanted to look, and I was incapable of thinking.

Mom knew that the sound of the vacuum cleaner bothered me. I knew this because over time she chose to vacuum my room last, with a look on her face almost like she felt guilty doing it, and she said sorry when she came in.

I couldn't interfere with Mom when she cleaned, though, *especially* not to ask her if she needed help. She wouldn't accept help. It just made her mad, because we couldn't clean as well as she did. It was best to get out of the way.

After the diagnosis, the hot sticky summer continued, and my days followed no pattern or routine. I lived the same day over and over again, and nothing really changed. I googled autism but didn't know what to do with what I read, except store it in a photo album on my iPhone. I found a lot of pictures and boards online that were about autistic girl traits, which was so eye-opening and validating. It was like being hit over and over with who I truly was. Learning that I was hiding—no, *masking*—my whole life made me feel misplaced. Every piece I read made me see myself as a little girl who felt real feelings but was taught to push them down, back into her bedroom, in the closet where no one could hear her. My heart broke every time I learned that I was always right. I had so many thoughts that I didn't know where to go. Most of my days, my head went off in all directions, and my body made motions to get through the hours.

It was a lot of just sitting on the couch, writing in my journal, trying to sort out the pieces. Mom was home one day, having a Wild Mom Cleaning Time and just frustrating me. She kept getting in my way and talking loudly and touching me and making horrible jokes, and I didn't react positively. I didn't react negatively either, but I didn't act like I liked it. Because I didn't.

I didn't laugh at her joke because it wasn't funny enough to invoke laughter. I moved away when she touched me without asking, like putting her hand on my leg or putting her arm around me or fixing my hair or adjusting my clothes. I might've previously played along like it was all fine, but it wasn't fine, and it had never actually been fine. I was aggravated, and I think she knew it. That made *her* aggravated.

It was after dinner and still light. The sky was lit with oranges and pinks, and I was in the living room. Mom came in with the vacuum cleaner and jerked it about in a way that made me certain she was in a bad mood. She was the most affected emotionally when we fought or argued or had any kind of issue going on between us, and it seemed her emotions were being taken out on the vacuum cleaner.

I sat on the couch with my right shoulder leaning against the arm, and I was zoned out and thinking. The sudden loud noise made my eyes freeze onto the cupboard below the TV, and I didn't make a pose. I didn't grab a book or a phone and pretend to be occupied. It wasn't because I didn't want to; it was because I *couldn't*. My brain couldn't move as fast as it used to, and I couldn't pretend. I had no energy left to pretend.

I wasn't really good at deciphering the looks on people's faces. But I knew Mom. I could only see her out of the corner of my eye, but her demeanor was simple. She didn't trust me. She didn't believe that the vacuum was actually bothering me.

She stopped vacuuming, turned the machine off, and faced me.

I had a feeling about what she was going to say.

"Ever since the diagnosis, you've been different," she said.

Yeah, that's what I thought you'd think.

"Oh," I said, still unable to move my eyes.

"Like, what, you've never had a problem with the vacuum. And now you suddenly do?"

"I've always had a problem with the vacuum," I said firmly.

She looked at me like I wasn't even her kid. It was like I was some random stranger, like I was purposely trying to be deceitful. She thought I was capable of that. She thought, if only for a second, that what I really wanted was to deceive her.

> Maybe I am different. Maybe I am acting differently. I'm just trying to be more myself. I just learned that all of the things I hate, all the things I don't want to do, I don't have to do them anymore. I learned that I was pretending all these years. Trying to be someone I never wanted to be.
>
> The mask is off.
>
> I don't have to hide or avoid or pretend or act to go about my life.
>
> The vacuum is loud.

> *You've never had a problem with the vacuum before.*

> Yes, I have. I just haven't said anything. Because who has problems with the vacuum? Everyone is supposed to be okay with vacuuming.
>
> And doing the dishes.

My eyes filled with tears and my face got hot.

"You've been acting more and more autistic since we got the diagnosis," she said.

She didn't believe me . . . She didn't get it. If only she knew how real everything was. The vacuum cleaner wasn't just loud; it was fucking mind-numbing and made me feel like my head was caving in, and I couldn't take another minute of being on this planet where Mom vacuums and I want to rip the plug out of the wall and jump up and down on the vacuum cleaner until it can never rage against my nerves ever again.

I hate it when someone thinks I'm a liar.

It makes me feel powerless.

Mom stared at me, holding the vacuum cleaner. I got so built up, I struggled to find words. "I cannot be any different from what I am right now," I said.

"Really? 'Cause you're sure acting different."

"I'm reevaluating my entire life, and you . . . It's a Wednesday."

"That's not what this is about. You're being rude and mean to me and I don't deserve it when I've done nothing wrong to you."

"My entire life has been flipped upside down, and I'm going to need a minute. I don't think I'm being mean to you. I'm not being a bad kid or yelling or being disrespectful. I'm just really sad and confused and not as happy as I used to look. This isn't about you."

She started crying and switched on the vacuum cleaner. I sat there, also crying, but silently.

She vacuumed around me.

I do not like to feel out of control.

In situations like that, I will never let the person make me feel like I need to leave the room, no matter how uncomfortable.

She took the vacuum and left the room.

I thought everything was supposed to get better after a diagnosis. I wasn't expecting perfection, but I expected to relax a bit more. Even with the diagnosis and knowing why the vacuum cleaner bugged me so much, life still wasn't good. Gradually, in slow motion, every aspect of my life became a blur. I knew what was going on with my brain but not how to use it.

I never thought of a "cure" or anything of that nature. I never really wished I wasn't autistic, even when it got really hard. I also experienced all kinds of problems that came with being a girl, but I didn't want to be a boy. I just wanted to be *myself.* I just wanted to know how I could be the best version of myself, given what I've got.

I longed for a world that never ignored me, that took me by the hands and said, *Here's everything you need to know about how your brain works and what you can do with that information to work with your brain to create your most happy, successful life. We can tell you because we studied autistic people a lot and really care about your well-being.*

The mental health care system varies tremendously area by area regarding availability and adequacy. Whether accessible or not, a lot of mental health services are not free, even though Canada has a publicly funded health care system.

I didn't want to waste time talking to someone who couldn't give me anything in return. Instead of someone trying to tell me why I should be okay, I wanted to learn about why I wasn't and what I could do to help myself. I wanted to learn what techniques might work. But I didn't know how to find that. When my own family didn't know what to make of the diagnosis, how could I even begin to figure out what to do next? I needed to go somewhere with experts—somewhere like a hospital.

I wanted help and support. Grade ten hadn't started yet, but I figured maybe I could miss school and focus on living. I basically taught myself schoolwork anyway, and I actually would get way more done if I did my work alone in a room without anyone bothering me. I wondered about going somewhere else, outside of my home, somewhere I could get help. There, someone would feed me and come sit beside me if I had a panic attack and help me calm down, and I wouldn't have to worry about what time I woke up or went to bed or ate lunch or went to study hall or went outside, because all of that would be decided by the hospital and not me, which was good.

Online, Mom found the first psych hospital I ever heard of, called Ontario Shores. It offered assessment and treatment services to people with various mental health conditions, with inpatient care. It felt to me that this could be a solution: I'd survive, because people would be taking care of my human vessel, so I could take care of my inner self how I needed to.

Mom and I went one day, weeks after my diagnosis. It was incredibly hot and sticky outside. Inside, the hospital was very cold, and it made my sticky sweat chilled. I became really cold inside wearing minimal clothing because I had sweat buckets outside.

We were encouraged to enter the facility and walk around, touring it on our own before meeting someone at the front. The hallways were wide and bright, lit with natural light from glass ceilings and windows on the left side, which revealed an outdoor area filled with greenery and stones. It was much more homey than a hospital.

Mom and I walked along, making conversation. "Look! They have a good mapping system," I said. "This shows you where to go." I pointed to a clear sign. "And there are no fluorescent lights. They've done that purposely to . . ." I paused. Mom's shoulders were up high and she was looking anxiously all around. "To be more autism friendly, I think." I stopped talking.

A man down the hall behind us shouted something and we both turned. He was probably double my age. He wasn't wearing a shirt. Nurses came and grabbed him. He looked straight at me before they walked him down another hallway and escorted him away.

"You're not staying here," Mom said. "How will you get better here? Away from us? From everyone and everything you love, in a place full of complete strangers?"

I didn't answer. I liked the place.

We walked back to the front, where a tall, overbearing woman met us. She led us to her office.

As soon as we sat down, the first thing she said to me was, "I don't think you're autistic."

Did she study me before this meeting and felt qualified enough to make that statement, or did she just say hi to me and then think, "*Nah. Not autistic*"?

I looked over at Mom, who was stiff and stressed.

The psychiatrist talked for less than five minutes. "We can't accommodate you, because we work with mental health conditions, not neurodevelopmental conditions like autism."

FIELD NOTES

I have mental health conditions that aren't autism that could be helped too.

And there weren't any autism-specific Ontario Shores kind of places around.

We went home, having wasted a day. I was unhappy and confused and I didn't know if we were going to be able to go anywhere else next. What was the next step after a psych ward? Could someone help me?

Mom googled again and found Dr. Sharon, a psychotherapist who had a shop downtown and specialized in couples counseling and mood disorders like anxiety, depression, and OCD. Mood disorders *don't* include autism. It's not under that random umbrella wording that gives very little clarity.

Upon meeting Dr. Sharon a few weeks later, I thought she'd be really helpful. I liked her personality a lot. She was only maybe a bit younger than my grandma in years, but she definitely looked younger. She had a wide smile and long, gray hair and always wore pretty outfits that were easy to move around in.

That first time, I walked in and sat on a leather chair in her office, across from her. She sat in a chair in front of her desk. She wrote on a big ol' pad of paper with a pen. She looked me in the eyes a lot.

I looked back in her eyes too. At first.

I was so excited to go. I wanted to go. I wanted help and knowledge and someone to tell me how to be okay. I had faith in Dr. Sharon and her thirty-five-plus years of practice described on her website. Every Wednesday, I was so ready to go to therapy at lunchtime. I was so excited for the opportunity to learn something new and figure something out about me.

But the same thing happened. Every. Single. Time.

Maybe she just didn't know what to say, or maybe her line of therapy didn't know what to say, because it was never what I needed. She was one of those counselors who was really only there to listen and maybe offer superficial advice here and there. Advice that did not work for me. Advice like:

- Breathe
- Do yoga
- Meditate

"I see," she said, sitting in her chair, looking at me. Or, "That sounds really hard for you." Or, "I can see how that would bother you."

Yes, Dr. Sharon. And then what?

Each appointment, I felt like I was talking to a castle. Like talking to a brick wall, except someone powerful is inside and they can only sort of hear you. And as the fifty-five minutes passed, my faith and my will did too. I was beaten down by my own frustration. I became ultra-numb. Unresponsive. I made no eye contact. I had to build up enough strength and willpower and regulation in my body to nod my head occasionally.

In this state, my tears dropped like a leaky faucet.

The first few times I went, Mom sat waiting for me as I exited the office, ready to drive me back to school, as it had started up again. She asked, "How was therapy?"

By the fifth or sixth time, I said, "Mom, I don't want to talk about it, if that's okay," and started crying. She knew not to ask again. She drove me, and I remained nonvocal for the duration of Wednesdays. I looked down at the ground silently as I walked through the school, thinking so much that it wasn't thinking at all. It was like when you spin a color wheel really fast, and you think all the colors combined make one big, explosive, loud color, but it actually makes white.

My thoughts were white.

Blue. Pink. Yellow. Orange sticky notes. I had them on my ceiling, filled with quotations and rules to live by. I had a million sticky notes. I liked using them for to-do lists, important information, quotes, or anything else specific I wanted to remember. I needed a disposable, specific way to place one distinct statement separate from others and discard if necessary. I went into my bedroom and opened up the top drawer of my desk where my sticky notes were located. I drew out the blue ones. I chose a black ink pen. It freaked me out that I didn't know much about myself, maybe nothing at all. I tried to write one true thing about myself.

I LOVE TO DANCE

No, that didn't feel right.

I LOVE DANCING

No, that wasn't better.

I LIKE DANCE
I'M A DANCER

Yes, that was it. Good. That was a fact, not an opinion. Did I like to dance? Yes, right? Obviously. But then I was second-guessing. What was another fact?

I'M A GOOD DANCER

Better, but I didn't fully believe that was true. It was subjective. I decided to try a different subject entirely.

What did I really know to be true? I flexed my fingers, and grabbed another sticky note.

I ... AM ...
BLONDE
5'4"
UPSET

Okay, maybe start with . . . being affirmative and concise.

I AM A GOOD BALLET DANCER

Yes. I ripped it off and placed it on my desk. I ignored the parts of me that told me not to.

Which parts of me were significant and important in my life?

Perhaps the sticky notes did not have to be definitive; they just had to be in front of me so I could see them.

How did I know what was truly me, and what I had convinced myself I was?

I LIKE DANCE

I ripped it off, put it on my desk.

I LOVE KIDS
PINK IS MY FAVORITE COLOR
I'M A GOOD BIG SISTER

Sticky notes stacked up on my desk as the thoughts exploded like I was flipping through a picture book. Once I had my thirty-four little squares completed, I gathered them in my hands and rolled my chair over to the right of my desk to an end table. It was white with two drawers, lots of stickers, and leftover bits of gum. The knobs for the two drawers were decorated with painted pink and yellow flowers. The bottom drawer rarely opened because it was not on a track any longer and was very stiff. The top drawer was filled with things I no longer used: old books, old stationery, cards from past birthdays, artwork given to me by kids or students, artwork I had done, colorful barrettes I no longer wore but couldn't part with. I started placing the blue sticky notes on my bright orange wall behind the end table so I could look at everything all at once. There were so many that I had to go on my tippy-toes to stick the remaining few.

I looked at the notes in front of me and then began ripping them off one by one.

No, I don't like that.

No, I don't know if that's me.

I'm not sure. I don't know about that one.

I ripped almost all the blue sticky notes off the wall. Finally, I was left with one.

I LOVE KIDS

I closed my eyes so I could listen to my body, while flashbacks of kids in my life filled my mind. Bella from dance. Deina and Mya from the bus.

All those sticky notes I ripped off the wall lay around.

> **FIELD NOTES**
>
> I didn't know myself that well.
> I didn't know myself *at all*.

I made a decision. It was time to stop being "myself"—the Paige who'd done her best to be who everyone expected, who tried to be bubbly and popular and helpful and who hid her confusion and overwhelm as best she could. I was determined to meet the mask-less Paige. But that wasn't going to be easy. She was buried under layers. And other people *liked* masked Paige. They liked Paige who endured vacuum cleaners and who hid her real self. I didn't know how to begin.

My thoughts were exhausting. But one shone through all the others: I believed the diagnosis would show me a path forward, but I was more lost than ever.

CHAPTER 11

TWO STEPS FORWARD

projections

a lot of what people say
is a projection of themselves.
sometimes,
when you're clinging to hope and someone says to you,
"but everyone feels this way . . ."
it's because they feel that way.
it also means that
somewhere,
somehow,
someone told them that they shouldn't complain either.

MOM TOLD THE SCHOOL ABOUT MY AUTISM DIAGNOSIS BY email. One morning, a few months into grade ten, I was given a slip from the guidance counselor's office. I had an appointment, it seemed, but I didn't recognize the name of the counselor. Someone new, someone I didn't know, someone who wanted to meet with me.

Other than the administration at school, I kept my diagnosis a secret from my peers.

I didn't want others to know yet, like Max said. I wanted to know, first.

You're stressed right now and that's okay, I told myself, sitting in class, waiting for my appointment with the guidance counselor. *You're autistic; you're supposed to be stressed right now. You're not broken. You're autistic. You're not broken.*

Grade ten started, and patterns were being made. Other kids sat together in the cafeteria, played intramural hockey, volleyball, badminton, dodgeball, went to someone's house for lunch. There were friend groups, and I didn't have one. Max had one, and I had him. Sam and I still hadn't spoken. We were both in math together, but we sat on opposite sides of the room. Then, one day, she walked out of class with a red face, crying, and didn't come back for almost a year.

Through the grapevine, I heard that she was having a rough, stressful time, like me. I feared having to do something about it, and that feeling never stopped. She cut down on her dancing a lot too. She stayed enrolled in a few dance classes, even some competitive ones, although she missed some nights of class. But we didn't talk to each other even when she attended. The crack in our friendship had become a canyon.

We hadn't spoken in so long. I didn't know how to reach out to her. I didn't know how to ask what was happening in her life, or how to tell her I was sorry.

I packed up my bags and walked out of homeroom by myself. I walked along the busy hallway and went to my locker. Noise and chaos all around me.

I entered the guidance office. A woman with very short hair and a soft, smiling face sat at her desk. "Hi, Paige, come and have a seat."

I sat across the desk from her. She had two big monitors off to her left that I could only partially see, giving me a glimpse of what looked like a database of names. The blinds were closed, and in such a small room this made the lighting soft and not too bright. She had a form on the desk in front of her.

"What's that?" I asked.

"Do you know what an IEP is?"

"I believe I know the gist of it," I said. "But you should probably explain it, anyway."

"An IEP in an individual education plan," she explained. "The school board puts it in place to help those who may struggle in the current learning environment. This gives you accommodations to help you succeed in school."

I remembered hearing it before. Max's friend had an IEP. He got extra time on tests. Max had told me how helpful the extra time would be for any kid taking a test. But I didn't need that. "Okay," I said. "What do you think I need help with in school?"

"Well, we hear that you just got diagnosed with autism spectrum disorder. Your mom put it into your file."

"Did she?" I said. I thought of Mom writing "Paige is autistic" on a sticky note and sliding it into my file.

"It might be that you need to take more breaks in class, or have a longer period of time for tests and assignments. And an IEP makes it so the teacher has to accommodate you. Or maybe you want to go to a different room to write a test by yourself."

I had gone through most of my schooling without the support and was a top student, so I thought I was doing alright. "Do you want me to have an IEP? Is this *for* me? Why?"

"Yes, you get one now. You have autism and you deserve to be accommodated." She smiled warmly. "We're here to help you, Paige."

"I don't know what to say," I mumbled. "I'm on the principal's list. I have one of the highest averages in school. It makes me feel bad to have help when I don't need it for my success. I'm succeeding in school." I didn't feel I *deserved* it.

"Let's think about the parts of school that are hard for you. Are there parts that you wish you could change? What could we put in place that would make learning easier for you?"

"Well, yes," I said. "I'd love to be able to stand up when I write tests." I felt like I was going to fall asleep when I sat down, stressed, for too long. I wanted to move my legs constantly.

"Done," she said. She tapped a finger on the form. "That's easy. We can do that for you. Go home and write a list of everything you wish could happen for you at school to make school better for you."

Writing the list was really hard for me. Even thinking about it now makes me cry. I didn't know how to ask for help. But it came out looking something like this:

- I would like to be allowed to stand up when taking a test, because when I don't I get so nervous and stressed that I often fall asleep at the desk.
- I would like to be allowed to ask as many questions as I want in class, an infinite number of questions, in fact, even if the teacher is frustrated and losing their temper and wants to strangle me and get on with the class (I understand because it's annoying this may not be realistic, but you told me to write down everything, so).
- I would like to get class notes as early as possible so I can go over them in advance or postscript what happened in class my own way.
- Can I do group assignments alone? Please?
- I would like extended time on assignments and extra time on tests and exams.
- I would like to have the same desk all year and not change seats or seat partners.

- I would like to be able to leave any class, for any length of time, and have the teacher of the class trust I will come back when I am ready.

After I handed this list to the guidance counselor, we made an IEP. Everything I asked for got put into the plan. It's all legally supposed to be enforced in Canada, with different provincial rules. It seemed impossible to imagine that people might be able to help me, and I felt overwhelmingly guilty. I was allowed to do any group project alone, to have the same seat all year—in front of the teacher and the board—and to have no one sitting beside me.

Teachers were supposed to provide me with a slideshow of notes a week before class. Dr. Brown gave me the whole year in advance, so some teachers were amazing and fantastic. But others really didn't seem to want to follow the IEP. I'm a stickler for rules, and I reminded them that they had to follow the plan. But I hadn't told any of my peers, and some teachers got irritated with me, creating tension in a place that was already hard for me.

It was as if everything had changed and nothing had changed at the same time.

Maybe don't tell people for a while?

Grade ten had occasional glimmers of beauty. Max and I were still dating, some of the teachers followed the IEP, and my family and I had settled into an uneasy acceptance for the moment. I had become friends with a guy named Seb, who was smart and kind. A girl called Liv and I caught the bus together and slowly started to become really close. And my dance friends, Mack and Emily, filled each class with encouragement and laughter.

But my life at the time was still very hard. I cried to Max most nights, and I felt awful about it. My parents weren't much help. My stress grew and grew and my thoughts were: *This is who you are as a person. As a person you are flawed and you cannot survive in this environment.* As the months went by, I thought over and over about death. It seemed that nothing was going to get better. I wanted to enjoy life, but my brain never stopped.

Suicide started to feel like my only option.

In March of that year, there was a big test that all grade tens had to pass in order to graduate. I was stressed out because I had seven hours of dance on the Tuesday before, until 9:30 p.m. We were about to enter competition season, and my dance studio liked us all to be ready, especially the top-level older girls like me. I also liked to help the younger girls and volunteered to be an educational assistant during any breaks I had. I was stressed and exhausted that night because of the upcoming test, and mentally I was prepping to go home and study after. Because I was so close to tears throughout the dance classes all evening, I was in a horrible studying position. My brain was spinning, and that's hard for me to stop. During the dance itself, I could move my body and distract myself, but by the time dance was over, I was a mess.

Mom picked me up. It was dark outside, and the sky had no visible stars. I shivered a little in my coat, pulling it over my dance leotard in the cold night air. Mom kept the truck running, staying inside as I climbed in. I was tired and not able to be in masking-Paige mode. I felt dead.

"Hi," Mom said.

As I replied with a short hello, I could feel her irritation. She hated it when I dropped the mask; perhaps she still wasn't used to it. I couldn't understand why it was hard for her, but I wasn't able to pretend in that moment. Feeling like I had to be smiling, sweet, happy Paige made me angry. I looked over at her.

She didn't put the truck into gear. Instead, she looked back at me, perhaps waiting for me to say something else. Sensing that she was upset with me made me even more mad at her.

I didn't speak. It was her turn to speak. I'd done my part of the conversation.

"What?" she snapped.

"What?" I replied.

"Why are you being like that?" she pushed.

"Like what, Mom? I just got in the truck." I started to cry. Mom was the least of my problems in that moment. I didn't have energy for what she wanted from me.

"What's with the attitude?" she said. "I know you have a test and you're stressed. I'm only here to help you. You don't have to be mean to me."

In that moment, I could see myself as a child and as the version of me I was now. I could see all the times I apologized for being upset. I felt so small and powerless.

And I was done.

"I'm not being mean." My anger was high.

She finally drove out of the parking lot.

"I'm really trying not to be mean," I said. "I'm just upset. I'm sorry that you think I'm being mean to you. Today has been a really bad day, and I would just like to go home and not talk about it. And I'd like to study. Can we just have this conversation later?"

"I just want to make sure that you're okay. You've been off all day today. I'm scared, Paige. You don't seem okay."

"I'm not okay."

"Like, how bad? Are you going to go home and hurt yourself?" Suicide had circled in my mind since I was in front of that coloring book when I was a kid. It was all that I wanted to do, always, but I just hadn't gotten there yet. I was practiced and prepared, waiting for whatever night I really decided to give up. "Paige, are you going to kill yourself?"

"I don't know, Mom. I might." I couldn't handle the stress, and I planned to relieve myself from it. Killing myself was inevitable.

"We're going to the hospital, Paige. I don't know how else to help you."

"No, Mom, please, I need to study."

"I need you to be safe."

On the drive to the hospital, I sobbed hysterically. Mom cared at the worst times, when I wanted her to care the least.

The psychiatrist on call had vivid blue eyes and looked like my childhood gym teacher. He introduced himself as Justin.

My brain shut off and I followed him with Mom by my side. We walked for a long time, navigating the main floor of our hospital through hallway after hallway. I never realized the hospital was so long too.

We stopped at the very end of a long hall, and Justin opened a door to a tiny little room. The door swung inward, invading the limited space.

"You guys just have a seat. I'll be one second—just going to try and find us somewhere to chat." Justin motioned for Mom and me to enter.

There was a dark-blue love seat against the back wall. The door almost hit the couch upon opening, so Mom and I had to enter the room first before Justin shut the door, and then we could sit down. *How strange to put a couch in such a small room*, I thought. It looked so out of place and didn't seem practical. Honestly, it was surprising the room was used for people whatsoever. It felt like a storage room where they stored their random blue couch.

The only other furniture in there was a desk that was slightly too big, sitting in the right corner by the door. The walls were generic office beige. A long painting hung behind the couch, framed in gold. The painting consisted of thick swatches of dark-blue paint that lifted and curled off the page and made the painting seem interactive. You aren't supposed to touch art at museums, but I didn't think museum rules applied in the hospital, and the textured painting was begging to be felt. I ran the palms of both my hands evenly over the deep blue waves. They were rough and unmoving. It was an oil painting. Mom just watched me. "Does it have a raised texture?" she asked.

"Yes," I replied.

Justin came back in with a black plastic chair. He pulled the seat down to open it up, facing me, and I noticed a small rip in the cushion, likely from a button on someone's pants. He'd said he was going to find us somewhere else, but I guess they didn't have a room available, so we had to do intake in the broom closet, with an abnormally large oil painting dominating the space.

"Do you have a plan to kill yourself?" he asked.

With Mom in the same room.

"Uh, what do you mean, do I have a plan? If I were to kill myself, yes, I know exactly what I would do."

Next, he asked me what the plan was. He wanted me to describe in detail how I would murder a person in front of my mom— how I'd kill her fucking child. I replied, the words spilling out. "Doesn't everyone kind of know how they'd like to die? I'm sure you guys think, 'I wouldn't want to drown or die in a fire,' but I think the proper answer is no, you shouldn't have a plan mapped out of how you're going to kill yourself. But I do have a plan. For sure. And I'd appreciate not talking about it in front of my mother."

Both he and Mom silently stared at me as if they expected me to explain. But I couldn't explain. I had no more words. Not about this.

"I like the painting," I said to Justin, not meeting his gaze. Someone had to break the awkward silence.

"Do you?" he replied. "One of the ladies here painted that. She's got quite a few paintings hung up in different rooms."

"Does she do it for free?" I asked.

Mom chuckled a little. I felt that if it were just her and me, she wouldn't laugh at that. Mom doing that felt like she was the one masking, not me.

I let Justin and Mom have a discussion while I zoned out and thought about the English test. Until he said, "You don't look autistic."

I didn't think that statement warranted a response, but he looked at me like he was waiting for an answer.

"Alright," I said, pretty pointed.

"What do you think about that?" he pressed.

"Well, I think that's just dumb of you to say." I had a diagnosis. My brain went from numb to on fire. "I didn't ask for your opinion on my autism diagnosis. I'm here because I want to kill myself."

Mom glanced over at me, perhaps trying to say, *Hey, don't be mean to him.*

I hung my head and looked straight at the ground as thick tears built up in my eyes. My breathing became erratic, and I felt light-headed. Justin tried to offer some words of reassurance and a tissue, but I decided I didn't like him very much and so I didn't care about doing what he wanted. I lifted my hands to my temples, ran my fingers through my hair, and balled my hands in fists to grab the strands right at the root. I put my elbows on my knees to help stabilize my head so it could hang down without effort and I didn't have to worry about falling if I passed out. He said some more things, mostly to Mom.

"I fear if Paige leaves the hospital, walks out tonight, she might hurt herself. It would be safer to keep her for three days to a week for supervision until things settle down and we feel it's safe to discharge her back home."

FIELD NOTES

Nothing like this had ever happened before.

- Staying in the hospital?
- How could that even happen or help at all?
- I was supposed to go home and study for the test.
- It was 11 p.m. and no matter how much I studied, I wouldn't get enough sleep and that would impact my test scores anyway and make me grumpy and I wish I was allowed to study instead of dance.

Justin left for a long time.

Mom and I remained in the room.

"I can't stay in the hospital," I told her.

"You need help," she said. "Tests don't matter. Maybe this is what we can do to help you. Maybe finally this is going to be a breakthrough. Let's not worry about a stupid test when you want to kill yourself."

"I can't kill myself until after the test is done."

"When has school ever been more important than *you*? You have to be here, with us, alive, to do school." It felt like she was yelling at me. Her voice was stern. "You gotta do this, Paige. We'll figure it out with school. I'll call them. But you're not going to die. Not today."

Justin then returned with a nurse and a security guard. He stayed behind as we walked away from him with the rest of the team, and I never saw him again. I started hyperventilating and had a hard time walking without passing out.

The room they took me to was in the same hall but at the other end of the hospital. The walls were white. There was nothing, only white. No sheets. No pillow. No blanket.

"So you can't hang yourself," said Mom. She wasn't speaking to me, though. She'd just made a shocking discovery and couldn't hold it inside.

I was encouraged to get up onto the cot by the nurse. I wasn't capable of saying no. I was exhausted. I was mad and exhausted and defeated. I flopped onto the hard, cold bed, exclaiming at the sound of the squeaky fabric against my clothes. Mom held my hand or my head or my leg or my back or my finger the entire time and tried to tell me I was okay.

Out of all the things that could have happened that night, getting admitted was one of the worst. I looked up at the ceiling. Above my head was a vent. It had a wire cage over it making it inaccessible, but air still passed through.

Mom said that was so I couldn't hang myself, but that didn't make sense to me. It was definitely possible to tie something to the wire cage if you wanted to, and I'd argue the wire cage would hold a lot more weight than the vent cover.

But then it made sense: It wasn't so I couldn't kill myself. The wire cage made it so I couldn't *escape*.

The door to the room was never allowed to be even slightly closed as long as I was inside.

A security guard sat in a chair in the hallway. She was there to make sure I didn't hurt myself all night. She was directly in front of my door, in my face every time I opened my eyes. She sat, staring at me all night—or so it felt.

They wouldn't give me pillows or blankets. "You need to go to sleep," Mom told me. It was after midnight. "I'll go home and bring you pillows and blankets." She drove home to grab stuff for me (including the blanket I cuddled with), so I didn't have to sleep on a stupid empty cot. While she was gone, I texted Max—for some reason, they let me keep my phone. I guessed he was asleep, but I wanted to update him on my last few hours.

Max didn't reply.

Mom didn't say much when she dropped everything off. "Are you good?" she asked. "Do you want me to stay?"

"I won't sleep if you stay in this room. You should go home."

"I'll be back in the morning." She left.

I texted Max again.

> **Me:** goodnight.

Although the lights in the room were shut off, the room remained illuminated by the light coming from the hallway and intake station. The room never darkened. Nurses sat at the intake station all day and night, constantly talking. Sometimes I peered out the window blinds to watch the nurses. I recognized a lot of them, and I could tell they recognized me. That was the worst thing about living in a small town. I couldn't go anywhere without everyone knowing who I was and who I came from and all of my business. My parents were two of the most confident, social, chatty, fun people that I knew; they loved talking to others. No matter where I went, adults came up and touched my shoulder and talked to me about my parents, and they always seemed confused when I didn't wish to have a conversation with them.

But that night, what it meant was that I knew some of the nurses, and when I know people I feel forced to mask. Because they knew me when I was masking, I felt like I had to put that back on, so I didn't want any of them to speak to me. I didn't want them staring at me. I didn't want any other nurse to know that Johnny and Tracy's daughter was in a hospital room equipped with a security guard.

I had a panic attack shortly after Mom left, and the guard alerted some nurses, who rushed in and tried to calm me. One told me to open my mouth and put a little tablet under my tongue. She said it would help me go right to sleep. I took it happily. I fell asleep in minutes and was only awoken the next morning by a nurse checking on me.

I waited for Mom, and for next steps.

The hospital screened my parents for sharp objects, like pens and scissors and paper clips and other suicide tools, before they were allowed to enter the room to speak to me.

I didn't have to know that, but Mom told me when she and Dad came to visit the next morning after Graham went to school. I was surprised that Dad came. I didn't know how he was going to react. I think Mom was pretty spooked about the sharp objects question. Her blue eyes were noticeably red from crying.

They came in, a psychiatrist behind them. I didn't catch his name, but he was the one who decided my fate. He stood in the doorway, much taller than I was sitting on the sad, white cot. "We're going to keep you here for at least a week," he said. "And then see if you need to be transported somewhere else."

My heart jumped into my throat, as if to try and control my vocal cords and manipulate my speech. My face grew hot. My head filled with pressure and noise as I waited my turn to speak. The ringing was so loud that I couldn't pay attention to anything else the doctor was saying. The hot tears felt like comfort, like a hug for my face, and I let them hold me.

"I can't," I said, and then I said it again. Over and over and over. My heart took hold of my voice and, like a heartbeat, continuously spoke, "I can't. I can't. I can't."

Mom must have realized that this was my whole fear of coming to the hospital in the first place.

"I need to get out. I can't even be here now. I can't stay."

"Paige, you have to. How are we supposed to trust you?" the doctor said. He spoke in a cold tone, like this was just protocol to him. He didn't react to my cries. He looked at me like I was a checklist.

Rules and regulations within a rigid boundary usually made me feel safe, because it meant the same thing each time, which was reliable. Despite that, I could never apply lists to a human being, especially a child, especially a child in danger.

Fuck the lists. Fuck the regulations. Fuck this hospital with its security guard outside of my door, staring at me all night. And fuck the *no sheets, no blankets, no pillows*, how I couldn't even have a pen to write or study.

FIELD NOTES

All of this was to keep me safe, but in what world would this environment make me not want to kill myself?

Why would anyone want to stay here for any length of time?

Who could see it as a sanctuary, a place of rest, a place to regulate?

Keeping me safe was fine, but what about *me* wanting to keep me safe?

What about helping me so I'm not in this place ever again?

Why couldn't I get help for the long term?

The thing about this test was that grade tens all across the province took it on the same day at the same time. Then, if you failed, you took the test again in grade eleven. If you still failed, you had to take a literacy course in grade twelve and pass that in order to graduate. I didn't want to lose that first shot, just in case. "What about my test, Mom?" I asked, frantic. "I need to do it today."

"I called your school principal," Mom replied. "He said you'll be able to do your test next year."

"But what if I fail it? Will I get to retake it in grade twelve? But what if I fail that? I won't be able to graduate."

There wasn't a good scenario if I didn't do the test that day. Taking the test that day also wasn't a good scenario, because I didn't get to study all night and I was a crying mess and I was on drugs.

"We can let you go only if you're safe. We can't let you go if we think you are in danger of hurting yourself." The psychiatrist was not pleased.

"I'd really, really like to go. I will have a harder time in here than I will out there these next few days."

"Paige, you've been saying you want to hurt yourself."

"I have a test. It's in an hour."

"What about after the test? Will you want to hurt yourself then?"

"I don't know because I can't predict the future."

"Well, you can see how that concerns us, Paige."

"Okay, well, if I'm feeling like hurting myself, I'll come back. If not, I'll stay home." That wasn't a lie. I couldn't lie. No matter how much I needed to get out, I could not say something untrue.

The adults left the room to discuss what to do next. Time went by. The test happened and I was in that white room. I missed it.

My parents and the psychiatrist came back into the room. The psychiatrist gave me a prescription for the mighty sleeping pill I'd had the night before, called Ativan, which I was to only take during "emergencies." He also prescribed me Cipralex, which I was supposed to take every day. It's for anxiety, depression, and OCD. I didn't have a diagnosis of OCD, but he told me that I did, in fact, have that too.

When the psychiatrist left the room, Mom said, "Everything with school is sorted. Don't worry. This morning, before Graham went to school, we told him you were doing okay."

"You told Graham where I am?"

She opened her eyes very wide and lifted her eyebrows. "You don't think we had to tell him last night why his sister wasn't coming home, and why Mom came home so late? You think he hasn't heard you or seen you any other time when you're upset?"

I sat back, looking away from her.

"Let's get everything packed up. We're going to go home."

I blindly followed orders. The hospital was so awful, and I wanted to get back to my room. Maybe the medication was going to help. Finally. Maybe something would change. As hopeless as life felt, that was life without medication, and maybe with medication it wasn't going to suck.

"Dad will hang out for a bit so you're not alone. It's going to take them some time to get everything sorted with your meds and release papers. I'll come back for you once this is all done. I have to go to an appointment." Oh. Okay.

Then it was just Dad and me. He pulled up a chair and placed it on the left side of the bed, close to my pillow. I lay down and turned my head to face him until he asked me for a hug.

That was the first day I ever saw Dad cry.

He began sobbing when he hugged me. And then he said he got it now. "I believe you," he said. "You're serious. I'm sorry I didn't understand before. I didn't know how bad it was." He cried into my shoulder as he hugged me. I cried back. My feelings were complicated. I wanted to feel comforted, I always did, but I was angry. His words felt late to the party.

Max came by during his lunch hour. He came in much more happy and cheerful than my family was. He smiled, sat on the bed, and held my hand the way I liked it. Immediately, he started making jokes and being comforting. "The rumor is," he murmured, his fingers laced through mine, "that you got to take a different version of the big test in a separate facility because you're so smart. The government needed to test you on another level."

"Dude, that's amazing," I replied. We both were laughing. He knew how serious everything was for me, but he also knew when to cheer me up. Any bit of lightheartedness came from his deep understanding. Max was able to understand and help me navigate how frightening reality could be.

I did the test the following year with no problems whatsoever.

The morning after the hospital would have been terrifying if I could have been afraid for my life anymore. I had two medications: the everyday one (Cipralex) and the one for when I had panic attacks and needed to quickly relax (Ativan). Dr. Hallix called me to explain them to me.

"Don't take the Ativan unless you really, really have to," he said.

I'd already taken one.

"They are a controlled, highly addictive narcotic," he continued, "and I'm nervous that they prescribed them to you. I wouldn't, and I won't, refill them. You'll have to go back to that psychiatrist for more."

I didn't take another Ativan. Nine still sit in a bottle somewhere at the bottom of a white purse I carried around everywhere with me when I was fifteen.

I woke up and stared at my sticky notes taped onto my white bedroom ceiling, close to my face up in my loft bed. Different sizes and colors. Each sticky note had a quotation on it, something inspiring or beautiful or some kind of life motto. Rules to live by.

I was seeing colors. In the white, behind the sticky notes.

The notes were not coherent at this moment.

Whatever I looked at seemed to morph shape and size, coming away from me and toward me like a pulse, like breathing. Flashes of green, blue, and red danced in the stretchmarks of my misshapen bedroom door.

I got the motivation to get out of my room. I looked away from the moving sticky notes. I stumbled out of bed and tried to get to the door. The knob laughed at me when I reached out a hand, then turned yellow and lunged away, making me trip. After a quick sob into my carpet, I stood up and closed my eyes before reaching for the door handle.

It was the same in the living room. Mom, Dad, and Graham sat on various couches, all awake and staring at me and asking questions. I couldn't look at their faces; the way that they morphed was disturbing. I asked Mom to turn the news on the TV off. Once she did, I stared at the black within the empty screen, at the blank TV that was full of the most nothingness I could settle in. And still, the nothingness expanded and shrank. Darkness capsized around me and pushed away from me, showing its flashy stripes in a taunting, playful gesture. There was nothing I could do.

For the first time, I stopped being scared. I stopped being anxious, because I was defeated. I could either stress and fight about something I couldn't change, or accept that it was happening and that I had limited capabilities of stopping it. I don't know if I chose acceptance, or if the medication subdued me into it.

I managed to talk to Mom about the effect of the meds, although I can't remember what I told her. "Hopefully," she replied, "that will mellow out as you get used to it in a few weeks. If it continues to be a problem, we'll go back to the doctor."

We didn't expect me to feel like sunshine and rainbows immediately. I thought my body would adjust and soon the colors would stop. Soon they would sort out my brain chemistry and I would be a little bit more okay. I put up with the colors for the whole day, and the whole next day, and the whole next week.

I continued taking the Cipralex in the morning, but my head didn't feel any better or less numb. The longer my eyes remained fixed on something, the more it morphed out of shape. I looked away often. The same happened when I focused on my eyelids. Sleep was very difficult. Falling asleep felt like a chore. My white thoughts didn't choose sleep, or anything else. My body chose my actions for me. I fell asleep when my body said I had to.

No one in my family talked about anything that happened. They kept facts in their heads and didn't share them out loud with each other. They smiled and tucked the bad feelings away and acted like everything was okay. They were the ones with masks on.

I can't move through the awkwardness of a home that knows it's broken. I cannot pretend like everything is fine. That's too much for my body to contain.

Graham knew. I needed to go talk to him.

A few nights after the hospital, Graham was in his room playing video games. On his blue walls he had huge posters of hockey stars and clothing brands he liked. His trophies and medals for hockey were on the shelves, and the drawers under his bed were messy and disorganized. His floor was only clean that evening because Mom would go in to pick up his crap and stuff it in the drawers.

The lights were off in his room except for the light that beamed from the TV screen by the foot of his bed. He sat upright on the edge of the bed and aimlessly shifted through options for customizing his avatar. He wasn't in the middle of a game with other people, which was good. I could speak with him.

His blinds were open, revealing the deep, dark field outside. Anything that lurked in the night waited to lunge at any moment, toward the blue light in Graham's face, so I crossed his gaze to reach the blinds, which I turned upward.

FIELD NOTES

Mom always turned the blinds downward, but that way, the sun glowed in my eyes in the morning. She closed her own blinds by turning them downward, and the same to Graham's and mine if she touched them.

I always turned them up.

After saving our lives from the monsters outside, I sat down beside Graham on his bed. He glanced up at me a few times as I made small talk about the video game and the blinds for a few minutes. "Can we have a gross, serious, big girl conversation?" I finally asked.

"Yeah, what's up?" he said, shifting toward me and putting his controller down. He said it like he was waiting to say it.

I began crying. Of course I did. Crying was my next step, the next level to the conversation, the inevitable natural progression on the way to the point. I took a few seconds to compose myself; I didn't want to cry in front of Graham. I wanted to be strong for him. I looked up at him and met his eyes and the first words that felt good enough to say were, "I'm sorry."

"For what?" he said with a light, airy grin. "You have nothing to apologize for. Nothing at all. *I'm* sorry." And those words made him cry. I knew he was sorry that I was sad. That I wanted to die. The fact that he knew what happened to me, the fact that he saw all of my mess, wasn't something I was proud of.

"I'm so sorry that I have to take all the attention from Mom and Dad," I said. "I don't want to take up all the space."

He was thirteen. He sat on his bed. "I don't need that attention. I just need you to be okay. You need to be okay for me to be okay."

"I never wanted to take anything away from you. Not our parents."

"Then you're good. Because I'm fine."

I was so lucky to have him. He was so happy and cool, with friends and sports and his easy way of being in the world. "I love you, Grahamy." I hugged him and he hugged me back harder. When we pulled away, we both laughed a little, looking back at each other, embarrassed about being sad. He handed me a controller and, silently, we played a game on the Xbox. I didn't know how to play it and that was okay.

CHAPTER 12

MY HEART IS BROKEN AND SO IS MY BRAIN

over

i was done fighting,
for anything
or anyone,

especially myself.

the brain is made
to keep you alive
not to keep you happy.

MY DIAGNOSIS WAS AN OPPORTUNITY TO REFRAME EVERY INCH OF my life, but I didn't know what parts of my life were real. I still had so much to learn about myself and about autism, but at this stage, everything had to *stop* first. I couldn't fake it anymore. I had to break up with the old version of me in order to leave her behind. That breakup wasn't going to be easy. It needed time and attention, and I needed support. It felt like every day I tried to meet myself;

the people in my life tried to remind me who I used to be—who I pretended to be because I thought that was what *everyone was doing* to survive this world. I *only* knew masking Paige, and that's who everyone else knew too.

In a movie, this change in me could happen in a few visual scenes, perhaps. With dark music and imagery, the film could convey the depression and pain of my experience. But the reality of shedding myself was excruciating and lonely. I became more and more unhappy, and this unhappiness made me numb for a long time.

It's difficult to share this time of my life, not because of how depressing it was, but because I actually don't remember much. I can recall eating sweet-potato baby food, seated in front of the TV watching *Teletubbies*, before Graham was even born, but I can't remember much of the last years of high school. I don't have an exact start and end date to that memory loss of my life. I don't know when I'll get it back, if I ever do. But if there weren't pictures of me onstage during a performance, or getting my driver's license, or going to the fair, I would not believe any of it had happened.

I was a zombie.

I didn't smile or sing or skip or say hello to anyone I knew in the halls or dillydally or worry about what other people thought of me.

I was overwhelmed and constantly cried as I roamed the halls. I sobbed over my schoolwork.

I knew it was bad, because I didn't even want to be perfect in school anymore. I didn't understand concepts, but I kept going without asking for clarity, even if I cried. I let my marks slip (below a ninety-five put me in a frenzy, so the eighty-four I have on my transcript haunts me).

I had so many feelings on the inside. I wanted to die, and at the same time I wanted to work on staying alive and fight for me and my relationship with Max and my family and my schoolwork and dance and life—all the while figuring out who I even was.

My desires all contradicted each other. I could take 360 different steps in different directions and none of them were correct, so I took none at all.

I was trapped inside my zombie body, roaming the halls with dark eyes and a temper.

I don't know if it was the medication that created the blackout or if it was the depression. A prolonged experience of depression can register as trauma, which can create memory loss. Seb jokingly made fun of me to help me through it, saying I was a hummingbird, vibrating, because my legs bounced up and down so visibly quickly that they blurred. My pupils were huge. One day, a teacher asked what was wrong with my eyes.

"Oh, don't worry," Seb replied. "She's just high."

"SEBASTIAN!" I cried. "No, I am not!"

The teacher laughed, and Seb laughed, because everyone knew I wasn't the type to get high. It wasn't funny to me at first, when I thought he was serious, but it was kind of funny. I nudged him with my arm.

One day, my weight-room teacher talked to me about my heart rate during an exercise, because my heart rate was very high and didn't recover quickly at all. My body was set like that, on fire, ready to go, all the time. I was a zombie on the outside, but on the inside, I had so many colors spinning around.

It was the first day of school in grade eleven when Max and I broke up.

I hadn't seen him for a few weeks, which was unusual but purposeful. I decided I needed to break up with him. It wasn't a healthy, happy relationship anymore. I couldn't get over past arguments, I couldn't leave him alone, and I knew he was unhappy and getting ready to move on.

Max and I went out for lunch. We walked to a local coffee shop and waited in line, the warm September day all around. I refused to meet his eye.

"Paige, talk to me," he said. "Are you breaking up with me?"

"I can't do this, Max," I said.

He was silent. I could tell from how his body went still that he was shocked. But I didn't want to look at him. I couldn't.

"Do what?"

"Us. This. I can't be your girlfriend anymore. I love you and probably always will. I'm sorry."

He waited as if I might say more. I wondered if he was still going to buy me lunch, because I didn't bring any money. It's funny what you think about in these huge moments of your life, the way the world keeps spinning. I kept my blurry eyes forward while his stayed fixated on me, like we were the only two people in the world.

"Paige? Seriously?"

I didn't reply. This breakup was quick because it needed it to be.

Max scoffed and walked out quickly, and I stood there in the line, weeping. This heartbreak was for the best, I told myself. An old man asked if I was okay. I didn't reply. I walked back, alone, to school, to my next class, without food and without a boyfriend.

Max and his friends scolded me as I caught up to them walking to class—the friends I once almost considered mine, too, because I hung out with them sometimes with Max. I looked down at the ground and pretended not to hear them, but I acknowledged their physical presence when they passed by, because to completely ignore their gaze would show I was purposely trying not to look at them.

That night, I cried and cried and cried. Alone in my bed. I reminded myself that the feeling would only get better with time. And I told myself that for three years as I got over Max, until it actually became true. It was a very tough time because my feelings for him were so intense, so vivid, so hard to let go.

FIELD NOTES

Did I make the right decision . . .
or lose the love of my life?

Just after Max and I broke up, a friend of mine and I were walking to class. She got mad at me because I missed her social cues again. She wanted that to change. I don't know exactly what I did that had made her so annoyed, but she stopped walking.

In order to explain to her why I'd got it wrong, I wanted to say that I was autistic. I wondered if I told her—it was the truth, the only thing that made sense—then perhaps she'd understand. She'd forgive me.

Maybe just keep it to yourself.

I took a deep breath. I was going to try this. I stammered, "I'm autistic."

"That's no excuse. That doesn't change anything," she snapped.

I thought it did . . . I thought it was supposed to.

I felt stupid and worthless and confused.

Days floated by, not like in a dream or a daze, more like a party I wasn't invited to, but I could imagine everything that was going on. I walked to class with a binder and a purse. Teachers taught school. I was a student.

Dr. Brown was my chemistry teacher every year in high school, and she became protective of me. I made my personality well-known to her throughout the years. She wasn't scared to try to nurture the curiosity within me.

"I see so much of one of my family members in you," Dr. Brown said. We were in the science lab, between long white desks, posters of equations and experiments on the wall behind us. She added,

"He gets flustered like you do sometimes, and if everything can't stop right there with him and wait for him to catch up, more starts to pile on top and pile up and pile up until it gets too much, and he explodes. He has to pick up the pieces from scratch and doesn't know which to pick up first and gets flustered all over again."

She suggested that, when I hit a wall, I back up and focus on my breathing for a second or two before locking in again. I was to do this when we did something I didn't understand that made me frustrated and cry.

"When you get all flustered and confused like that, I notice it, Paige. If you can't understand something and you start to get stressed out, you either figure it out, or your brain stops. It hits a wall. When that happens, you aren't going to do your schoolwork successfully. You have to stop doing your schoolwork. You reach the point where parts of your brain shut down to focus on keeping you alive. How are you supposed to worry about schoolwork when your brain isn't? You can't work on what's frustrating you until you are calm and ready to try it over again. When I say that to you, I need you to hear me, take the cue, step back, and focus on you. Not the work, just on you."

"I can't do that," I said carefully, because I was already getting flustered at what she'd proposed.

"Paige . . ." Dr. Brown pleaded. "Don't hit a wall right now." She meant it. "As much as you want to learn everything, right then and there, you simply can't."

I was long past hitting a wall. I was one with the wall. A lifeless space, a vast, empty mind with dead eyes behind chipping drywall.

Grade eleven was a year when I felt like nearly every person actively hated me. But the one good thing that I had was what we called G7. This meant that I was elected onto our school board, made up of the seven high schools, with a student from each school going to board meetings. I loved that. It was important to me. And being voted in for that role mattered to me. At the end of that long, bad, grade eleven year, I ran for G7 again for grade twelve.

I saw Snapchat stories of girls in the cafeteria taking videos of the other candidate, captioning it that everyone should vote for her. There were multiple photos and videos of support, showing off the candies and cookies my opponent handed out as part of her candidacy. All of those people were Max's friends. They were girls who I'd hung out with before. They were girls who I thought I could consider as my friends too. They were girls I thought were for sure going to vote for me, or if not then at least vote for the other girl *secretly*.

One boy in my science class posted a photo on Snapchat of one of my posters, made fun of it, and told people not to vote for me. He'd posted it twenty-two hours ago, so it was going to disappear in two, and most of his friend list had already seen it.

"Jeez, Liam," I messaged. "I didn't know you felt that way? This really sucks to see from you." I felt like I needed to throw my phone across the classroom and set myself on fire.

"Aha I'm so sorry Paige. Nothing personal against you, I just don't like the meme on the poster. I'm still gonna vote for you."

I didn't respond. There wasn't anything to say.

He didn't delete it. He let the timer run out after twenty-four hours.

I felt small.

I lost the election. We two candidates found out in the office alone before an announcement was made to the whole school. After I found out I lost, I didn't want to walk back to class. I wanted to stand in the office and not move until I knew which way to go next. But I walked out, toward my locker. School had fifteen minutes left.

An announcement rang out announcing my opponent's win as I walked back to my locker. A small group of girls hollered in the common area far behind me, in the direction my opponent walked in after leaving the office. "Woo!" They clapped and cheered her.

"Fuck you, Paige!" A voice rang out in the crowd. I didn't even recognize who it was. Who hated me that much that I didn't even know?

FIELD NOTES

The truth is, a lot of the people who voted for me the year prior were friends with Max.

About a month later, I ran for another political placement as vice president of the student council. I made up new signs for a new campaign.

HEY! ME! RUNNING FOR SOMETHING ELSE!

PAIGE FOR VICE PRESIDENT FOR STUDENT COUNCIL!

I didn't win that election either. That was a big fat L in front of the whole school. I detached myself from the whole experience. I threw out any and all evidence of my campaigns. I quit the student council and the school play. I had to forget.

WHAT IS FUNCTIONING?

I know an autistic person who is primarily vocal. They can maintain a singular occupation for an extended length of time. They have friends, they go out to bars and restaurants and concerts, and they can drive a car. They smile. They say, "Hi, how are you?" when they see someone they know across the street. They can stand in front of people and deliver a speech. They can tie their shoes, make themselves coffee in the morning, and take their garbage out every Thursday. They are what some would consider "high-functioning."

I also know an autistic person who has meltdowns every day. They can only wear specific kinds of fabric because most feel uncomfortable, like fire on their skin. They have difficulty discerning physical pain and can have broken bones and infected organs without even knowing. They also register temperature poorly, and without assistance can dress dangerously inappropriately for the outside weather. They have poor executive function, which can cause them to be incapable of completing even the simplest, most mundane tasks, like brushing their teeth, eating, changing their clothes, or cleaning their body. Sometimes they can only communicate by nodding or shaking their head. They wave and clap their hands often; they repeat phrases over and over again; they wear earplugs in public and can't go to the grocery store alone. Allistic people could consider them to be "low-functioning."

Both of these people are me.

As we saw in the diagnostic criteria, there are no guidelines regarding functionality of an autistic person. Because it's an abstract idea, there isn't a diagnosis. There isn't a list or a category, so if someone tried to make one, what exactly separates high-functioning and low-functioning into a dichotomy is subjective. Behavioral functionality is another social construct without concrete rules.

Some say they would consider an autistic person low-functioning if they were nonvocal. I've heard some say they classify a high-functioning autistic person as someone with the ability to live alone. I've heard that the distinction is in reference to if an autistic person can cook, if they can work a job, if they have friends, if they can drive, and about a dozen other tasks or concepts. It is not universal, and it has no bounds. To me, that means that the concept isn't valid. These opinions are not based on facts, and therefore I cannot accept them as an opinion that I deem important.

I have been called high-functioning more than I have been called low-functioning. I am typically called high-functioning by people who don't know me, or by people who only see videos I post online. I am a unique, ever-changing human who is never 100 percent high-functioning and never 100 percent low-functioning. How well

I function varies tremendously depending on the situation and will vary tremendously for every single autistic person.

What if an autistic person held a job steadily for the last ten years, although they communicated with augmentative and alternative communication and couldn't drive a car?

What if an autistic person needed someone to take care of them with eating and cleaning and safety, but was primarily vocal and rarely had meltdowns?

What if an autistic person was at risk of putting themselves in life-threatening danger every day if they were alone, but they were able to be social and had a lot of friends they did lots of activities with?

If someone describes an autistic person as low-functioning, what would you infer that person needs? Whatever that answer may be, the truth is going to vary from person to person. On the flip side, I can tell you that often when people hear "high-functioning," they assume that means the person doesn't require help or assistance. I know, from my own experience, this couldn't be further from the truth. This misconception left me to struggle alone for a very long time.

So, not only do I think that these labels are incorrect and unfair, but I also think that they're useless.

I've heard people use the phrases "high support needs" and "low support needs," but I think the way they're used is pretty much the same as the functioning labels. And I also think they are still way too vague to be able to provide any real, actual, accurate support.

I just think it's impossible to separate a group of such unique and diverse individuals into one of two categories. It doesn't serve any valuable purpose in our lives. If the point is to disclose what a specific autistic person needs help with, the best way is to simply do so.

I think it's also important to add that the idea of high and low, and the basis around functionality, primarily compares us to an allistic default. Why? That would raise the question: What does being an allistic person mean, and what would make an autistic person closer to being an allistic person? What is it that allistics do, that only some autistics do, but most don't?

And is the answer "work"?

How well can an autistic person perform tasks that are important for having a job? How likely is it that this autistic person is going to be able to make someone else money? Are they a team player, or should we worry about them because they stir the pot? Is there a high chance that we will not need to think of them as autistic, because once someone is working their output is all that matters? Or is there a high chance that they cannot be ignored because they have a low chance of fitting into capitalist society? How likely is it that this autistic person is going to be a nuisance because of their inability to provide monetary value? How likely is it that this autistic person is going to need a different system than the one that we've already built and wish to maintain? How much is this autistic person going to cost?

I don't think autistic people are good for capitalism, and I know that capitalism isn't good for autistic people. I would argue capitalism is only good for maybe forty people in the whole world. It's important to remember the world we live in today and acknowledge the systems that actively step on the backs of others to exist and thrive.

ASPERGER'S SYNDROME

I do not use this term and haven't for many years. The DSM-5 does not recognize Asperger's syndrome as a diagnosable disorder. The American Psychiatric Association used to, though, in the DSM-4 (a previous version).

When I was diagnosed in 2015, my official diagnosis was autism spectrum disorder. However, my psychiatrist made sure to clarify that I'd be diagnosed with Asperger's syndrome if were still in existence.

I was autistic, and I have always been autistic. Asperger's is autism. If you have Asperger's syndrome, you're autistic. That is just a fact. Once I really started to understand that, I could begin recognizing my own internalized ableism, and why I used to prefer using "Asperger's" rather than "autism."

I know a lot of people originally diagnosed with Asperger's who still use that label today. I think everyone's own internal experience is true to them, so I don't care to argue otherwise. It's good to feel understood.

Learning about why Asperger's syndrome even existed was a solidifying factor in my autism acceptance. With many scientific discoveries, the person who made the discovery (or at least the person who had the best publicity) sometimes had the opportunity to name it after themselves. Some examples are a Venn diagram, Halley's Comet, and the Fibonacci sequence. Anyway: introducing Hans Asperger.

Hans Asperger's character is up for a lot of debate today. Without making this a history book, he was affiliated with various organizations working with the Nazi Party during World War II and agreed with the idea of creating a genetically "pure" society, which led to euthanizing certain populations deemed inferior in order to ensure the "perfect" population. In Asperger's case, he specialized in autistic kids. Autistic people were among the so-called inferior portion of the population, and thus were included in the mass genocide.

Some say Hans Asperger could be considered a hero because he saved some autistic children. Some people are proud to bear his name to this day because they believe he made a positive contribution to autistic people, which, scientifically, I guess he did make a leap. And according to the history books, he really did care about these kids and they really liked him.

Asperger determined that within the population of autistic children, there were some who could be considered "viable." I don't know the criteria by which he decided a child's life was or wasn't worth living or sustaining. He spoke to each child and each family individually and made a decision on a case-by-case basis. Others were diagnosed with sociopathy and idiocy. Their parents were informed that there was no way to help them, and these children were euthanized or sent to places where they were. In this way, Asperger advocated for the children deemed to have what he later called Asperger's disorder and actively discarded children who didn't.

The entire notion of Asperger's syndrome came from deciding that some autistic people were more deserving of life than others. It came from an idea of superiority, from eugenics. From warped perceptions of society and worth and what was good and what was bad, ultimately rooted in capitalist notions that children with Asperger's syndrome could find a job and "fit in" to their idea of a perfect future society.

This infuriates me.

FIELD NOTES

Your worth isn't determined by anything.
You are worthy because you are here.

I don't think this dichotomy of separating autism from Asperger's should've ever existed. I don't think it has any need or merit to exist now, and upholding the Asperger's idea and terminology also upholds the idea it was built upon, which is that your autism is acceptable only if it is invisible.

A lot of people don't know where this term came from and perhaps don't see the harm, but as someone who does know, I can't push that aside or forget about it.

All in all, I'll never refer to myself as having Asperger's syndrome ever again.

As grade eleven continued, I started hanging out with an older guy I met through a family friend. This was shortly after Max and I broke up. This guy had graduated high school and worked full-time at a company his dad owned. He had a car and could hang out at any time, which was strange and new and cool, considering that before, Mom had to drive me into town to see Max.

We started spending time together and making cookies over at his house, but I wasn't sure what was happening between us. One night, he texted:

Him: Are you seeing anyone else?

Me: no im not seeing anyone else.

Him: So then basically you're my girlfriend.

Me: oh?

Him: Yep. That good?

I came out to the living room and told Mom, "So, I think I have a boyfriend now." She didn't face me. I told her everything, and I wanted her to say something, respond somehow. Maybe to tell me she thought that was nice or be happy for me. Or be mad at me for having an adult boyfriend when I was only sixteen.

After twenty long seconds she didn't reply. She stayed on the couch, not looking at me.

I went back into my room and shut the door.

stupid little girl

some men seek out autistic girls.
autistic girls who don't know
who they are
or what they like
or what they're supposed to do.

no one has ever made me feel
as much of a goddess as he did.

My parents had no idea what to do with me as the year progressed. I changed in a way they didn't understand and didn't enjoy, but to be fair, neither did I. I was reconstructing my whole person while also dealing with intense heartbreak and limerence and battling the side effects from my medication, all while having two avoidant parents who couldn't help themselves, let alone me.

I set boundaries for the first time, which my parents thought was plain rude. I started saying no. I checked out of unproductive conversations. I stopped spending vast amounts of time explaining myself. I conserved my energy.

Mom seemed really mad at me, but I didn't care. By that I don't mean I didn't care about my parents. I mean the meds made me feel both here and not here, like I was participating in my life while simultaneously being an observer on the sidelines, knocked out and foggy, watching someone who looked exactly like me going about her life. Mom was working long hours, and it seemed like she was always on the phone. She was short-tempered and quick to blow up. It felt like she was always yelling about something.

Mom protested this new version of me. But I wasn't going to suck up my emotions to make Mom feel any better. I couldn't even if I wanted to.

FIELD NOTES: SCATTERED

Walls don't have emotions.

Maybe just keep it to yourself.

I told the new, older boyfriend that I was autistic a few months into our relationship, during a fight where I felt I had to clarify, to explain. He said the same thing as the friend I told after I broke up with Max.

It doesn't change anything, and it's no excuse.

I kept getting deflated.

Me being diagnosed autistic was supposed to change things.

One rainy night, my older boyfriend and I were driving in his car. I was sitting in the passenger seat, texting a friend of mine, the dark slipping by outside the window.

My boyfriend didn't like this friend of mine. He was a very jealous, protective guy who didn't know how to trust anyone or relax.

We drove on this winding road, the tension between us rising.

"I know you're texting Savanna," he said. "Stop it."

"No. That's not something you get to tell me to do." I spoke in a monotone. I was emotionless and burned out. He didn't seem to care. I didn't care either.

The tension rose.

I texted my friend still.

He swerved his car to the right, then to the left fast, and my head bashed against the passenger window.

"What the actual fuck, dude?" I said. "Did you just *intentionally* hurt me?"

"No, I didn't!" He looked over at me.

"Did you just intentionally bash my head against the window?"

"Whatever, Paige! Get the fuck out of my fucking car!!" He pulled over on the dirt road. "GET THE FUCK OUT!"

I had already unbuckled my seatbelt and had my mom's contact card open. I stepped out of the car and pressed "call" before I even closed the door behind me. I walked a few steps closer to the ditch as he continued to yell from the car. Mom answered after one ring.

"Hello?" she said, nervous. Mom knew what I was up to because I kept my location on for her. She and I weren't in a good space, but I still never went anywhere I wasn't supposed to, and it relieved some of her anxiety to know where I was.

"Mom, can you come pick me up in the rain in the middle of nowhere? My boyfriend swerved to bang my head on the car window, and I think I have a concussion. Now he's kicked me out of his car."

He began screaming behind me. The window was down and he yelled at me, feet away. "BABY! BABY, NO!"

I said, "I'm on the side of the road."

"What the fuck, Paige?" she said. "Yes. I'll be there. Where are you?"

"Come back in the car, please!" he shouted. "Please, I'm so sorry! I texted your mom and told her not to come get you because I'm not leaving you. That was a joke. I'd never leave you."

"Mom," I said. "He's trying to talk to me. Hold on."

"Paige!" he yelled. "Please get in the car. Please, baby, let's go home and talk about everything. I'm so sorry." He started to cry. He was so small, and I felt for his pain in this moment: the trauma he'd been through as a child—which I won't share here—was visible to me. I saw a hurt and scared boy who needed a hug. I pitied him.

"Paige?" Mom asked. "Paige?"

"I'll be fine," I told her.

". . . okay?" Mom said. I could tell from her voice that she was concerned, but I didn't let our conversation go any further. I hung up the phone. I looked into the car at his sad face for only a moment. I didn't care about anything anymore. Then I climbed in and said, "Don't talk to me. Drive me home."

Mom didn't ask about it again.

I didn't break up with him for another couple months, though. I knew I shouldn't have been with him in the first place. My mind cycled only through thoughts of suicide and Max and trying really hard to stop both those thoughts. It was only a matter of time until I was beaten down enough to finally end things in a dissociative haze, like what happened with Max. The day I broke up with him, I didn't plan it. I was so unhappy, I blurted out, "I'm done." Instead of being in a line for coffee, like I was with Max when I ended things, I did it in his running car, parked in my driveway as he dropped me off from a dinner date he just paid for. I don't even know what I said, and I felt guilty, but I was so relieved when I went inside the house.

I *tried* to pay for the dinner.

He was really upset when I ended things. I felt horrible, although I couldn't understand why he felt so strongly about the breakup. It was obvious he didn't even like me that much.

Mom was really not vibing with unmasked, depressed Paige. She was angry with me a lot. She looked at me like she expected me to say something, all of the time. She played some game in her head she thought I played too. She acted like any other girl at school who didn't like me.

I. Did. Not. Care. I said things to her like, "You're my mom. Can you please just act like a mom? And do mom things? And comfort me and love me because I'm sad and that's what moms do?"

She looked at me, puzzled, like I didn't make any sense.

I wasn't doing anything wrong or bad or stupid. I just didn't laugh at her jokes, and I didn't pretend to be okay when I wasn't, and I didn't fight with her when she wanted to fight, and I didn't say what I didn't mean. I was done trying to read subtext. I was done guessing how someone felt.

"You can speak to me like an adult," I said, one afternoon in our living room. "I'm not guessing your thoughts or feelings. It's your job to communicate them with me."

But she just didn't understand. If she felt insulted, she checked out of the conversation.

One morning, we were both in the kitchen trying to use the Keurig, her to make coffee and me to make tea. We bumped into each other a little, got in each other's way. Mom said I was grumpy and had an attitude and was mad at her and ignoring her. Dad came into the room and must have sensed the tension.

We bumped into each other again. Mom yelled at me, like good, for real yelled at me. I cried and ran into my room. Then, I overheard her telling my dad that she refused to be my mother if I was going to be like this.

Maybe she thought that would change me.

As part of this refusal, she didn't talk to me, drive me to dance or work, make me lunch, say goodnight or goodbye. She made that decision herself, to take a giant step back, so I respectfully collaborated and gave her space.

Sometimes she said something about me to Dad when I was in the room.

As if I wasn't there.

It sucked for sure, but it wasn't going to work on me the way I suspect she wanted it to. The way that it would work on her. I think the biggest hurt for Mom was feeling out of control and unable to do anything to help. She made a statement that relinquished all of her control and took away all her help.

But I didn't need a chef or a chauffeur or a maid or another gift. So it was fine, just annoyingly passive-aggressive.

The fight that changed it all

Mom, Dad, and I talked about that fight later. Mom highlighted how important it was to her. Baffled, I asked her, "What was so significant about that to you? What did I say? What did you say?"

"I thought you were going to punch me right in the face," Mom said. "Or tell me off and swear at me or spit in my face or something."

"I thought I was about to break up a fistfight," Dad added.

"What the *hell*?" I said. "*Why* would you think I would do that?"

"I thought you were mad at me."

"Do you even *know* me?" I asked. "Do you know who I am? You thought when you yelled at me, I was going to punch you in the face? And *not* cry?"

"No, clearly, I didn't know you at all," Mom said. "That was when I knew it. I knew I didn't understand you. What I thought was an angry feud was actually me hurting my baby girl."

I began crying and she continued, also crying. "You were so sad and confused and your world was upside down and you needed your mom to lean on but I abandoned you."

Back then, it was nearing the end of grade eleven. April or May or June. Brain fog. I had my driver's license and my own car and was able to drive myself around alone. The snow was long gone and the world was green and thriving. I was just trying to get through the days.

There wasn't much Dad loved more than loud noises. Music and concerts and playing drums in a band were huge parts of his life. He had a sound setup that he continuously upgraded every time he found a larger speaker, displayed in the basement with lots of seating for his guests. The living room floors shook under my feet. He laid back, relaxed in a leather armchair with eyes closed, and enjoyed a deafening amount of Judas Priest, Led Zeppelin, and Metallica. I often closed the door to the basement out of some kind of noise-dampening hope. When I was younger and I finally did go down there to ask him to turn it down so I could sleep, I ran down with my fingers in my ears and kept my request brief. That was until he built a garage double the size of our house on our property sometime before I was ten.

He dedicated the entire second floor to his band's setup, creating the most calculated surround-sound system. His chair sat in the middle of the room because that was where all the speakers met, he said.

FIELD NOTES

Dad was like the anti-Paige.

Dad also loved the purr of a '69 Chevy Camaro and the ripping of rubber against the asphalt when the tires spun and smoked and smelled. "What's the point in driving a cool car with the windows up?"

My hair smacking my face disagreed. I didn't need wind at that speed in my hair or in my ears. I rode on our snowmobile or four-wheeler with him with my fat, ear-covering helmet on and played music through earbuds. Dad hooted like a frat boy tearing up the fields. Loud noises were *really* loud. I couldn't understand how anyone could listen to fireworks without plugging their ears. I hated emptying the dishwasher. Cutting the grass. The clanking of the plates, the droning of the lawnmower, anything electric is noisy— the sounds were grating.

- I heard the constant buzzing of the fridge.
- I noticed the sound of lights, particularly big overhead fluorescent lights.
- From outside, I heard my phone vibrating inside the house.
- I woke up in the middle of the night when the dishwasher ran.
- I heard birds' wings flapping, coming from far away, which meant that I'm really good at duck hunting.

I wasn't good at hearing people, though, and often didn't respond to my name when called. Sometimes it took a minute to translate what someone said from sounds into photographs in my mind that meant something. I frequently mixed up letters and numbers audibly, like remembering that *yew* was *U*.

That April, May, or June day, I drove home from somewhere, dance presumably. It was still light outside but the sun was low. I parked down by Dad's shop. He wasn't outside, which was unusual. I grabbed my stuff from my car and locked the car door behind me as I walked up to the house. He met me halfway there. He must have seen me pull in through the window. Mom's truck was home.

I didn't look at his face, to indicate that I didn't want to initiate conversation, but he did anyway. He was a block in my path to the front door—if he didn't move, I had to go all the way around Mom and Dad's trucks and that was awkward.

He spoke. "Paigey." Always Paigey. "Mom's really upset, hon," he said.

"I don't know why, Dad. What have I done? Seriously? What have I done?"

"I know, babe, and she can be so sensitive." He was talking funny. "All you have to do is just say you're sorry and this will be done."

"I can't apologize for doing nothing."

"You're right, and you know she has a hard time seeing things from that perspective like you and I . . ." he chuckled. He tried to make us seem the same, and Mom was the weird one. She was overreacting. But did he tell her that? Definitely not, or else he wouldn't have been where he was that day.

"Me," I affirmed. "She doesn't see *my* perspective. You're not on my side."

"I have to be on your mom's side. She's my partner."

"And I'm the kid you built because you wanted one. You're not gonna choose me? I choose myself. Figure it out, Johnny." I strutted by him and went inside, being careful not to slam doors and give Dad a reason to scream his head off. I didn't start to cry until I reached my bedroom and shut the door, and then I sobbed uncontrollably in my closet, to try and dampen my noise.

About a week later, my parents caught me in the living room alone and cornered me into a family conversation with just the two of them.

I didn't know why we had to talk, or what the conversation was about, or what the problem was or the desired solution or my fault in all of it. I shut down completely. We came out of that moment and Mom was more okay and decided to be my mom again. She said she was going to attend a few of my therapy sessions with me, to better understand me and work on our communication. She spoke with Dad afterward, quietly in their room, to sift through everything. I heard mumbles from down the hall as I stared at my English binder in my room. Mom left the conversation with a changed perspective. I left the conversation as a black hole.

Through all this, I continued going to therapy with Dr. Sharon on Wednesdays during my school lunch break. Dr. Sharon didn't really get me. My brain was foreign to her.

At my next appointment, Mom led the way into the room. I took one chair, and she took the other. Dr. Sharon looked over her glasses at us. "Well, hello both of you. How can we use our time together well today?"

The three of us exchanged the most awkward eye contact, trying to figure out who was going to speak first. "I just want to be here to learn more about Paige," Mom said. "I want to listen in so I can support her best."

I sat silent for a moment.

"We don't know how to communicate," Mom added.

I remained silent. The two of them talked as if I wasn't in the room. They were laughing together, connecting, chatting. They were on the same level. "What's difficult about the communication?" Dr. Sharon asked.

"Paige is difficult to talk to."

"Why?" I asked her. "Why is it difficult to talk to me?"

"I have no idea," Mom said. "Paige is mean to me a lot of the time." She turned to face me. "I feel like you don't like me."

"That's not what this is about at all," I said. "That's what matters to you right now? I'm sorry you think that, but I do not think that's our problem."

"Well, what do you think our problem is then?"

"That you don't understand me at all. When you talk to me, you're yelling." I cracked my fingers with my thumb, one at a time, on both hands simultaneously. "And when you're not, you're always busy and working. You're always on your phone. That's why you don't know how to talk to me. You're not talking to me."

"I don't yell all the time." Mom leaned forward in her seat. "I'm not always on my phone. You're wrong. I'm always here for you and not always working long hours."

"Why is it always table tennis with you? Can you try to not be offended at my true experience, and just accept it and not try to make it a fight? I feel like you took a long time to even see there was a problem," I said. Suddenly we were having the Big Conversation that had been looming and building momentum. Heat and resentment. "And now we have an answer, and you've left me. You still have no idea how to comfort me at all."

"I honestly didn't see any problems, Paige," she said. She turned to Dr. Sharon, then back to me. "I saw you had problems, but I didn't think it could be autism or any of those things. I didn't even know much about what autism was, anyway."

"You don't know much about it now," I said.

Dr. Sharon leaned on one hand, listening.

"I don't think that you verbalized what was happening to you very well," Mom said.

"Mom, I'm still a kid," I pleaded with her. "How am I supposed to know what's up with me? Or that there's something wrong, or different? This is the only life I've had. And there hasn't been enough of it yet for me to know what's typical and what's not."

Mom started to cry.

"It's not my job to know what I need," I added. "It's yours."

Dr. Sharon was quiet, monitoring us opening up and getting real.

"I always thought," Mom said, tears rolling down her cheeks, "that people treated you differently because of your overwhelming talents."

"I know! Because you don't see my experience as separate from yours and how girls treated *you*! I always knew that if everyone else felt the same way that I felt, there would be a lot more kids killing themselves," I said.

Dr. Sharon intervened to say to Mom, "Do you see any problem with her diagnosis? Do you struggle to believe that Paige is autistic?"

Mom looked shocked. "No," she said. "Are you kidding me? No." She looked over at me and then looked down. "No, not at all," she repeated. "Not one problem. Everything. Boom, boom, boom, check them off the checklist, or whatever, because that's Paige. Like, it explains everything. It explains everything, don't you think, Paige?"

Pause in the therapy room. No one spoke. It did explain everything, but I wasn't going to let the conversation be sent off to me.

"I thought you were perfect," Mom said into the silence, "just how you were. The way you are. I'm sorry."

CHAPTER 13

NOW I HAVE OPINIONS

kintsugi

in order to put
myself back together,
i needed to figure out
which pieces of myself
i wanted to keep.

MOM BEGAN TO CHANGE THE WAY SHE INTERACTED WITH ME. THE more confident I became in my boundaries, the more I upheld them and respected myself, the more she learned about my needs.

She didn't get it right a lot of the time. But holy shit, she never stopped trying. As we went through the summer after grade eleven, there was a shift in my family life. And I knew, too, that grade twelve held promise. Graham was going to be in the same school as me again.

Graham and I hadn't been in the same school since I was in grade six, which was now six years ago. A lot had changed about us. We were pretty stoked that our age difference made it so we'd be together once more before I graduated.

I was nervous to be in the same school again. Excited and happy, but also very nervous. I knew that I wasn't popular. I was not even necessarily well-liked. I wasn't cool. But Graham was.

Not only was Graham cool, but he'd instantly get cooler in high school because he was so good at making friends. He could read people very well. Graham did not fear change, nor did he fear new things and new people in new situations. He didn't walk into a room and wonder if everyone in that room was going to like him or not. Graham was excited at the opportunity to meet new people. He was good with them.

I had already established a reputation. There was no scope for reinventing myself. And now, my younger, cooler, and taller little brother was about to show up and see what my life had been like at school for the past six years.

I really wanted him to think I was cool. When he got invited to parties that people my age threw that I wasn't invited to, I drove him and his friends there and back. And when Graham and his friends started failing math, I was the one who tutored them. I gave what I could offer, which was mostly just responsibility. He was at school, making lots of friends, getting invited to every party, walking the corridors in squads, handling pretty much all social groups in all social settings.

Graham got taller and more popular, and soon he was the cool sibling. Kids my age and older who never interacted with me invited Graham to hang out with them. Graham didn't care much about school, so he had a lot more free time than I did.

One day, after grade twelve had started, I was crying to my mom about how I had no group of friends, and this obviously meant everyone hated me, because there was this party that I wasn't invited to and everyone else was and it made me feel like a loser. Mom and I were both standing in the hallway, and Graham was picking some of his clothes up off the floor in his room with the door open.

Graham chimed in. "Paige, you literally hate everyone who's going to the party. Like, why do you care?"

I was so thrown off. "I hate everyone? No, I don't!" As I understood it, I loved everyone.

"You do hate everyone, Paige," Graham said, walking into the hallway with a T-shirt. "You don't want to be friends with any of them, so why do you care about this party at all?"

His words made me think. Why *did* I want to go to this party?

"You don't *have to be* friends with everyone," he added.

"But you're friends with everyone."

"We don't have to be the same. You're not *like* everyone else. You don't have to want to party every weekend," he said. "You don't have to care about whether or not those people include you. Why would you want to be included? Would you have fun there? Seriously. Think about who's going to be at this party."

Max would be there. I didn't want to talk to him or see him. None of his friends even liked me and they'd all be there too.

"It's a high school party," Graham concluded and bent down to pick up a baseball hat. "It's not a big deal, okay? You're gonna be freaking president one day or something, and that's gonna matter way more than getting drunk every weekend."

And that cold shower of common sense is what brothers are for.

"You're focusing on all the wrong people," Graham added, looking at me and pausing. "Who do you like? Go be friends with them."

Graham was right. It was time for me to stop viewing myself from everyone else's perspective. It was time that I started caring about my own. I wanted to get to know unmasked Paige, but I didn't know *how* to do that.

The me I created wasn't from my perspective. I'd been cosplaying as a person: a little person inside of me worked all day, analyzing, collecting data, while my body provided information.

I saw me out of another person's eyes. I put on a show, and I was the performer and the director.

FIELD NOTES

- That feeling of constant stress, of hypervigilance, the conscious but seemingly uncontrollable analyzing of my surroundings
- The snapshots in my head from times I remembered that impacted me so deeply
- The times that I held back, and said yes even though I really wanted to say no
- A puppet master, that's all I was. All I *really* was, anyway.
- So small. Underdeveloped.

I had worked vigilantly on constructing a life that was not mine for a long time. By doing this, I created a made-up life, convincing myself that I liked it. On and on it had gone, this charade, this magnificent piece of theater, the Paige show, where I watched how other kids my age seemingly glided through their lives without difficulty, without stress, winning friends and smiles and approval in the classrooms where we spent our long days learning. I played a character, a composite of all their social successes.

I knew for months now that I needed to figure out who I was: Graham's words showed me why.

That grade twelve year, with Graham in grade nine, really created a shift in our relationship. For the first time, my younger brother got to see that his older sister, the one who'd tried to teach him how to read when he was four months old, was vulnerable. He knew for years that I struggled, but now he was there with me, watching me.

A lot changed as the shock and awe of getting diagnosed with ASD settled down. I found I could accept help from people more easily, whether that looked like a student offering to explain something to me in another way, or taking a tip on leggings versus jeans from a popular girl while getting changed for gym class.

I also noticed I was becoming more accommodating. Less rigid. Less black-and-white in my everyday life. I could bend a little to accommodate Graham or my mom or my dad. Flexibility had never been on my radar before, but now I was able to see that there wasn't one way to do things.

I asked questions whenever I needed to. And I informed all of my teachers that I'd ask fewer questions if they sent me the lesson plan beforehand, allowing me to look over it before coming to class. If they couldn't do that, then I asked to be allowed five minutes at the end of class for a quick question firing from my list. (This was in my IEP, so the teachers had no choice but to allow me to ask as many questions as I wanted. I was just being courteous about the method.) Some teachers wouldn't send me the materials even a day beforehand because they didn't want to remember to, and they also didn't want me to hold them up for five minutes after class. And to those teachers I thought, *You asked for it.*

All realities are true
There isn't one answer.
When people ask me about terminology
and how to refer to autistic people,
the best I can do is give my opinion,
which is just *one* opinion.

ABLEISM

My opinion is based upon the facts that I have and can't be understood without understanding ableism. Ableism is, in short terms, discrimination against disabled people. As someone with autism, among other disorders that severely impact my life, I consider myself disabled. I believe that what disabled people think about disabled people's issues is the most important, if not the only, opinion worth considering.

Ableism comes in many forms and in various degrees, but the fundamental underlying tenets are usually these:

- Believing disabled people are lesser, which we looked at in the section on Asperger's. Disabled people were euthanized during the Nazi regime—obviously that is an extreme example, and ableism is less advertised today.
- Believing disabled people shouldn't be alive. Examples of this would also be Nazi times, or how disabled people in some US states are denied organ transplants, or when fetuses with Down syndrome can be aborted at an older gestation point than other fetuses.
- Believing that ableism isn't a problem because disabled people aren't as important and therefore do not need to be accommodated. Any place someone in a wheelchair can't access or a classroom where a kid who is neurodiverse doesn't get support (not allowing iPads or service dogs) would be examples of this.

There's never a time when I, a disabled person, need to be corrected by an abled person regarding how I refer to myself. There isn't a time when an abled person can tell me that I am wrong about me. Of course, it's important that everyone learn about ableism whether you're disabled or not, and educating others on ableism should not only be a disabled person's job. However, I don't find it right or fair to ever correct anyone regarding how they would like to be referred to, in any form. That's an individual choice and should be respected.

Ableism is built into Western society. As ableism is one of the pillars our society is built upon, it can be unsafe for disabled people, especially intersectionally marginalized disabled people, to not comply with their own oppression.

Disabled people can have ableist beliefs, which is called internalized ableism. Every disabled person is in a different place, in a different situation. We don't all have the safe and healthy space to explore and unlearn our own internalized ableism.

Around one billion people are disabled right now. That being said, that leaves more than 80 percent of the population as abled people who are likely unaware of the privileges they experience. It's easier to get jobs, to make money, to find housing, and to find others to accept you when you are not disabled, as basic examples.

This system is so much a part of our lives that we don't see it and can't imagine dismantling it to make it fairer for everybody. The idea of dismantling oppressive systems can be overwhelming for most people because the majority benefit from the systems in place. So, by default, they don't even see that there's anything wrong. This can be because of an unintentional or even a willful ignorance.

I don't believe in being ignorant. I believe ignorance is one of the worst traits a human being can possess. I'd like to think that human beings are not evil so much as they are just uninformed, and if everyone knew the hardships others experienced, they would want life to be different too. But I think that lack of knowledge separates us. To change a system, you have to first know that there is something that needs to be changed. Looking at my own history shows a list of possible changes just in the autism realm: for example, better investment in mental health supports and better education for teachers and other students. We have the ability and the resources to help people but often decide that some needs aren't worth helping.

WORDS, LIKE DISABLED

Phrases such as "differently abled" and "special abilities" are really condescending and imply it is wrong or bad to be disabled—or else why wouldn't you just say "disabled"? Of course I am differently abled; I am, in fact, able to do plenty of different things. I have tons of abilities too; I don't know which ones are so "special." But I am also disabled. There is no need to dance around the word "disabled" if you do not think it is bad to be disabled. Disabled is not a bad word.

Disabilities exist. People are disabled as we speak. Actually, most people will become disabled one day, if they live long enough. You will likely be disabled one day from disease, old age, an accident. Would you like people to pretend you weren't?

Some may say, yes, they would like people to pretend. But again, is this because of ableism, because they'd prefer people not see them as weak, or less intelligent, or whatever they negatively associate with being disabled? If your ableism is stronger than your need to survive, I understand why this could be the case. However, we cannot deny the fact that a disabled person is disabled, whether they accept it or not, whether they want to be or not, and whether they are accommodated or not. I have always been autistic, before I knew I was and still today. I always will be autistic, no matter how accommodated I am or whether others decide to ignore that. I believe it is best to accept reality and accommodate as such, rather than pretend that every person is the same and has the same abilities.

There's this underlying sense that I need to be "abled" to be better.

Let's think about it like this: A person with shaky hands would not be a good brain surgeon, a person allergic to cats would not be the best veterinarian, a person with a fear of heights probably wouldn't be a helpful skydiving instructor, and a person who doesn't speak French wouldn't be an effective French teacher. It is humanly impossible to be completely self-sufficient and to assume all roles. Everyone has their strengths and their weaknesses.

Would you tell the shaky-hands brain surgeon that she doesn't have shaky hands and could perform brain surgery just as well as everyone else?

Would you tell the sneezing vet that he is not allergic to cats and could be around cats just as long as everyone else?

What about the skydiving instructor who has a fear of heights. Are they as fit to be a skydiving instructor as someone who *doesn't* pee their pants when they look out the plane window?

Would you say a non-French speaker could teach in French just as well as people who speak French?

Hopefully not. Because people with these characteristics could choose different occupations, as they hopefully have talents and interests in other areas. That doesn't mean these jobs would be impossible with some accommodations: an app to help speak French, allergy meds for the vet. But that doesn't mean a person should struggle wherever they are. *We aren't supposed to be able to do the same things.* Yes, I should be accommodated during tests, but also, maybe tests are ineffective!

I believe it's wrong to treat every single person the same way. This is why the public education system bothers me immensely. Every single person needs different instructions and support to excel, and there should be absolutely zero shame in having help in certain areas to allow someone to have the best life possible. I believe that is what we should strive for in education, because collaboration and cooperation is the way society functions.

Now, being disabled is not the same as being allergic to cats, but I wanted to use examples of things people cannot do to help drive this point home: disabled people are not able to do some things, and *not being able to do some things is okay*. It is not helpful to believe that disabled people can do everything an abled person can do. That is quite literally the whole point of the word. There are some things I am simply disabled from doing, and the sooner everyone accepts that, the sooner I can stop putting myself through hopeless, helpless attempts to do so. I accept what I cannot change about myself. There are some things I cannot do no matter how hard I try.

Please do not pretend I'm not disabled. Please acknowledge that I am and help accommodate me so that my life can be easier in a society that was built without my needs in mind.

Back in grade twelve, before I could figure all of these things out about the society I lived in, about the complexities of being disabled, I had to know *who I was in the world*. And while my conversation with Graham changed things for me, it was still two steps forward and lots of steps in confusing other directions. This path wasn't easy or clear.

I wanted to tell people that I was autistic, even if they didn't understand.

I didn't want to hide anymore, and I was ready to be seen.

I forced myself out into the world, places like the dance studio where I went despite longing to be home with my head under a pillow or in a blender. I wore whatever the heck I wanted, pulled my hair out of my face, took all my makeup off, and drove myself to dance without a seatbelt on. I turned on the windshield wipers and turned up the music and drove really fast.

Sam became friends with the other girls our age in the class. They were once my dance friends, but now they were Sam's, even out of dance. One girl who I was closest with told me that Sam was having all of the dance girls over except me, and I got really upset. I was upset with that friend, too, for going. She didn't really talk to me as much after that.

And then I was mad at everyone at dance who hung out without me all the time. So, I went to dance and I focused on dance. I barely spoke. I focused on my mind–body connection and becoming a better dancer.

They laughed and giggled around me, and I just worked harder.

I loved dance. I loved having my body to focus on. I loved being autistic during it all, so I didn't care about the other girls or what they did. Only me. By myself with my body in a room, moving, rocking, swaying beautifully.

I enjoyed the younger kids at dance because they had so much energy and talent. They couldn't stand still and just *had* to dance, like I felt I did. These kids were easy for me to talk to and understand.

Bella and I had a couple of duets that we competed with over the years. The dances were fantastic and emotional and beautiful, but my bond with the little bean was what really made the dance magical. I'm so thankful to be in her life still today. I think she sees me as an older sister.

At the dance studio, I was me, without constant awareness of what that meant to other people. But I still had to deal with the girls my age and older and the teachers. One afternoon, with the light like honey over the wooden floor, bouncing off the floor-to-ceiling mirrors, a teacher, Naomi, ran our hip-hop class. Sam was there, too, and every time I asked a question that night, Sam answered.

I didn't care to listen to her. I didn't want to say that, though. I just looked at her, nodded, and said, "Oh, thanks," and turned my focus again on Naomi.

However, Naomi's explanation wasn't useful. I still wasn't understanding the move. Naomi was out of ways to explain it.

"It's okay," I said, trying not to get frustrated. As the year had gone by, I was getting better at regulating. I used social media for tips and breath work, which helped a little. I definitely wasn't learning anything from Dr. Sharon, although I still went every week. "Let me try it a few times," I continued, "and I'm sure I'll figure it out."

Sam spoke again. Maybe she was trying to be helpful, but our friendship was so long dead that I just wanted her to stop interrupting. She offered no new information, no new way of thinking. No benefit whatsoever.

Naomi moved to one side and said, "Thanks, Sam. Maybe if you show the move, then that will help?" She gave Sam the floor and allowed her to continue trying to teach me the dance move. I think Sam was just being herself and trying to help, perhaps thinking she knew the golden-nugget piece of information I needed to make it click, but she didn't.

"I thought Naomi had her right foot in front, not her left," I said. My throat was tight. I stepped back and focused on being in the moment. Trying to regulate. "I'll figure it out. I don't need you to—"

Sam kept going. "You just put your foot like this," she repeated.

"Can we just stop?" I said. "Please? Sorry . . ."

"We're just trying to help, Paige," Sam said, her exasperation vivid and filling the room.

I wanted to say, *I know you are! I know everyone is always trying to help! But you're not! And I'm sorry I don't know how to say that to you in a way that won't make you feel like a worthless dumbass, so I keep my frustration inside and try to be as polite as possible, which will still result in my inevitable doom! Please don't try to make me feel like shit. Your help I didn't ask for isn't helping!* I said those things in my head, but they didn't come out of my mouth. I only nodded at Sam and attempted a smile and eye contact. Tears and rage filled my eyes but didn't fall.

"You don't need to get so mad at me," Sam snapped.

The words burst from my mouth before I could stop them. "Did you guys know that I'm autistic?" I looked around. My face got hot. I couldn't wait to see what they'd say. I'd stumped them; surely it would take a while before any of them could put their thoughts into words.

"Yeah," Sam said.

What?

"Yeah, I think we all did," Naomi added.

"How did you know?"

The studio director had told them.

I thought if people understood me, they would be better to me.

Sometimes people understand you, and they just don't care.

This was the response I was used to. It had happened before. But this time, I was a little stronger. A little older. Even if other people didn't care, I cared.

My diagnosis mattered to me. It was who I was. It explained my worldview. And if other people didn't understand that or care, then, as Graham had helped me realize when we chatted about that party, *why did I care about their opinion?*

That was on them. Not me. I wasn't going to stop telling people. They could do with the information what they wanted, and if that was nothing, let it be nothing, if only for the possibility that it *could* be something.

PERSON-FIRST LANGUAGE VERSUS IDENTITY-FIRST LANGUAGE

Person-first language is phrasing used to identify or describe someone by referencing their personhood before their disability. It describes a person as *having* something, instead of *being* something.

- Person with autism
- Person with blindness
- Person who uses a wheelchair

The main idea of using person-first language is to separate the person from their disability by making their identity only that of a person. The separation ensures that you are not making the disability the person's identity. This idea is heavily enforced in academia and medical settings, primarily in fields where disabled people are a common community—for example, those who treat disabled people, like doctors, teachers, nurses, and social workers. It is so drilled into people that I will get corrected by nondisabled people if I do not use person-first language even when I refer to myself.

Then there is identity-first language, which is basically the opposite. Identity-first language refers to the person and their disability together, implying the person's disability is an intrinsic part of their entire identity.

- Autistic person
- Blind person
- Wheelchair user

I believe person-first language is straight-up, basic ableism.

Its creation and heavy enforcement implies that the opposite terminology, identity-first language, is problematic. And, because person-first language is used by people who take care of disabled people, "experts," it's supposedly believed that person-first language is the least ableist option.

I recognize that those who take care of disabled people likely want the best for them, or else they would not choose to work with them. But I seriously question if disabled people were part of this decision-making process at all, as we haven't been for much of what impacts our lives.

Identity-first language is not ableist and should've never been opposed.

I am autistic. I am always autistic, in every situation, all of the time, 24-7. My brain literally formed differently. Everything I do and everything I have ever done, I have done autistically. I would be a completely different person if I wasn't autistic, and the idea of who that person would be is something I could never figure out, because autism is such an integral part of my identity. To take it away would be to take all of me away, and I find it ableist to want to try.

The idea of person-first language separating autism from something that I *am* to something that I *have* tells me that it must be wrong or bad to be autistic. It tells me that it is better to have autism separate from myself than to be and identify as autistic. This comes from the thought that being autistic is bad, or lesser, or not desirable compared to being allistic—that it is something you want to separate from who you are. That's ableism. Autistic people are not allistic people who also have autism; we are never *not* autistic. We can never just leave our autism at home. Autism influences every single part of my life, making it absolutely part of my identity.

My other problem with person-first language is the idea that referencing a person by the fact that they are a person before their disability is supposed to be good. Somewhere along the line, someone thought, "Man, being autistic means not being a person." Somewhere, somehow, someone decided they needed to refer to me with the word "person" first, so they could remember that I am one, so I can be grateful that they still see me as a person *despite* being autistic. Someone somewhere thought they were such a good ally by creating this language that would finally bring humanity to disabled people.

No one should have to use the word "person" first to remind themselves that, although I am disabled, I am still a person.

This again comes back to ableism. I believe this act of confirming personhood before the disability is because the disability isn't seen as being part of a person but as something that distracts from a person's humanity. It seems as though the basis behind this language is to think it is bad to be disabled, that it is better to have a disability than to be disabled, and that it's harder to recognize someone who is disabled as a person.

Sometimes it works better in a sentence to say "people with autism" or "autistic people," and I often use them interchangeably without a second thought, because it shouldn't matter. I will never make a distinction to only use one over the other, because they both serve a grammatical purpose. But the idea of *only* using person-first language, specifically for the reasons that person-first language was designed, is ableist and makes me feel very uncomfortable.

When I was in grade twelve, Graham's friends (although not Graham) went through a phase where they started using autism as an insult, like how people used to say "that's so gay" when something wasn't cool. They started saying, "That's so autistic." I heard it quite a lot before I finally said something. I recall one of my brother's friends using that phrase when he meant something was dumb.

At that time in my life, if I was confident in one thing, it was that I was not dumb.

We stood in the kitchen in our house. Graham's friend ate a watermelon slice. I remember saying to him, "Do you think I'm dumb?"

"No, of course not. You're the smartest person I've ever known," he replied.

"Oh, well, I'm autistic, so I think you need to get a better adjective."

He paused with the watermelon held in front of his mouth. "You're not autistic, are you?"

"Yep, I sure am."

Graham smiled at me.

And I never heard any of my brother's friends say that ever again. That's when it really hit me: *autism was me.*

I started to feel more comfortable *as myself* with some of the other kids during grade twelve. Seb and I had lunch together often, chatted together, texted, and hung out after school. He was also excellent to debate against in class and out, and we became best friends.

One day, we got into a loud and passionate discussion in class and had to be reminded numerous times to sit down. Neither of us noticed ourselves rising from our seats when we had to share a perfect piece of information to combat the other's side.

We reconvened after class by my locker down the hall. I made a face at him when he approached, a face that meant, *I just totally owned your ass in there, but good game, and I'm glad we're friends, douchepants.* I put my hands up to add to the gesture. It looked proper.

He and his friends laughed. Seb split off from his crowd to stop and talk to me.

Something about the way we interacted in that debate room had lit a match inside me. Seb and I knew we were quite similar; we actually made a list of similarities we shared between the two of us. But now I knew he was even more like me. And I felt like I needed to tell him. I needed him to know this essential part of me.

"I'm autistic," I said.

"Uh, ya."

"What do you mean 'uh, ya'?" I said, frowning. This wasn't how this conversation usually went. I did not prepare for this response.

"Uh, ya, of course you are. That sounds about right."

"What?" I repeated. I put my hand out onto the locker next to mine. It was cool and hard.

"What, did you think I didn't know?" Seb scrunched up his nose.

"Did I tell you before?" I didn't think I did, but I couldn't understand why he was being so casual.

"It's just obvious." He smiled warmly. "And I'd like to think that I'm your best friend, Paige. You'd think I know a thing or two about you!" With that, he took off down the hallway to his next class. I watched his first few steps, and then looked back to my open locker. I smiled really hard. *He knew.*

Someone knew. And accepted my autism as me.

I started to tell people more and more. Sometimes people were shocked when I said that I was autistic, and I loved that. Sometimes, it changed the way people thought, because me being autistic was a fact, and so no one could argue. If they tried to argue that I wasn't autistic, they were wrong and therefore their opinion was invalid to me. That gave me a kind of power, because I had knowledge that the rest of the world seemingly didn't have yet: that I had an autism diagnosis and autism could look like me. I could teach people about ASD, if they wanted to learn. I had information.

And that made me excited.

Dr. Brown was a killer biology teacher, as well as being great as a chemistry teacher. She sent me lesson plans, presentations, slide-shows, and homework all in advance. I came into every class know-ing what was being taught that day.

Dr. Brown didn't mind me staying behind after class, where I'd get five minutes to ask all of my questions. I wrote them on a sticky note (or ten) during the lesson and stockpiled them for those golden five minutes when I had Dr. Brown all to myself.

It turned out when I sat with questions sometimes, I figured them out on my own.

If I needed to scoot, like if I felt overwhelmed and hit a wall, I simply put a pink sticky note on my desk and left to go to the bath-room right across the hall from the science lab. I didn't have to ask Dr. Brown for permission because she trusted I'd be safe and come back as soon as I could.

In grade twelve, I was on the ballot for valedictorian, just like in grade eight. I wanted that so badly. Being grade twelve valedictorian was a dream I had through elementary school and high school. On voting day, I walked to the office at lunch to place my vote. A friend stood in front of me and placed his vote into the ballot box first. As he turned around and saw me, he blurted out, "I voted for Jamie, by the way. Not you. Sorry." He laughed and walked away.

Paige by the end of the year in grade twelve had a little bit of a sense of self-identity and boundaries, so I actually said, "What the fuck?" out loud to him, so he knew it was a conversation now.

He stopped.

I started, "In what world is that a normal thing to say to anyone, let alone a friend?" He faced me and looked like he was going to talk, but I was not going to listen, so I said, "No, literally fuck off, Trent. You knew this was something I wanted so badly and you're a fucking prick. Leave."

And I turned around, disregarding his response, checked my name on the motherfucking ballot, and put it in the box. I turned to walk out and didn't even look to see the expression on his face.

Trent's friends surrounded him with their mouths agape, and they did not say a single word.

I smiled as I walked down the hall.

One night, I was scrolling through my feeds when I read something that snagged my mind.

> You have one trillion cells in your body and each and every one for their whole life just work on keeping you okay and alive and healthy.

Reading that felt so visceral to me. Despite how badly my brain wanted to die, my body never stopped fighting for me. It clotted my blood when I bled. It would make me cough or throw up if I were to take too many pills.

My body wanted me to stay alive.

FIELD NOTES

You know what, brain? If you want to kill me, you're gonna have to do the dirty work yourself. Trying to make me do all of the hard work for you while you just get to sit back and relax? Come on, kill me like a real disease. Infect me, shut down my organs, dehydrate me, do *something*.

The last few days of high school in grade twelve were just for fun, basically. There wasn't new material being taught or any class that really needed attending, but there were events for seniors.

It turned out Dr. Brown quilted in her spare time, and every year she made as many quilts as she could so that she could give them away to some of her grade twelve students before they graduated. She did it like a raffle, where she gave every student two small pieces of paper and had us put our names on them. We put the slips in the raffle for whichever quilt or two we wanted.

I cried when she brought them out and told us the idea. It was the sweetest gesture in the whole world. We could tell it was special to her. She welled up with tears presenting them to us.

There was a smaller pink quilt she specifically pointed out as she went through the ones she made that year. "Now this one, I think, is *so* Paige." She glanced over at me and smiled. The class agreed—the pink quilt was *so* Paige—and some of them glanced over at me and smiled too. (I didn't even wear a lot of pink or anything. I think I just exuded pink energy.) I put both of my tickets in for that pink quilt.

She drew the raffle as soon as everyone had returned to their seats, satisfied.

When it came time to draw for the pink quilt, she made swift eye contact with me before pulling a name. She glanced at me quickly before reading it aloud. I knew from the way she looked at me, how her eyebrows didn't raise, that it wasn't my name. I knew Dr. Brown's patterns over the three years of teaching me, I knew what face she'd make if she saw my name. It's subtle, but I'm good at noticing fine details; most people are patterns.

Dr. Brown stuttered before she said the winner. There was a guy in the back who said it was his sister's birthday, and that's why he put his name in for that quilt. He was going to give it to her as a gift.

I was a little disappointed, but it was okay. It made me feel good just thinking that Dr. Brown may have wanted me to have one of the quilts she'd made. I decided that feeling was even better than getting a quilt.

Later that day, I stood at my locker getting ready to go home on the bus. I saw Dr. Brown's shoes come into my field of vision from the left, her yellow Crocs. I watched her last five footsteps toward me.

"Hey, Paige?" she said.

I turned to face her, making my attitude and body language seem almost shocked to see her and not like I saw her approach.

"Do you have a second?"

I didn't, because I had to take the bus and it was leaving shortly. So naturally I said, "Sure! What's up?"

She pulled me aside near the entrance to the staff room. "I was so upset when you didn't get a quilt today!" She threw her hands in the air and made a face.

I couldn't believe I was right. It was so nice to hear. I began to laugh in a light but friendly way, because I wanted to make her feel like I understood, and it wasn't a big deal, and I wasn't upset.

"Oh gosh, that's totally okay!" I said. "That's so nice of you to say that, and to think that."

"Do you like green?"

Oh. My brain connected the dots fast, zipping thoughts around my head, gathering clues to answer the question properly. The truth of the matter was I did not like green at all. I actually hated green. Green was the worst color out there. All the girls wore gross, army-green coats in the fall, which blended in with the drab ugliness of the mucky fall weather and looked sickly. Green had been my least favorite color for years. I knew that was the honest answer. But I knew it wasn't the right answer.

"I *love* green!" is what I said.

"Oh, good. I'm actually in the middle of making another quilt right now. It's almost done. I hadn't planned to have it finished before the school year was done but I think I could have it finished for your exam. It's just that it's green. Like, green, green."

I'd made the right choice.

"I just really want you to have one," she said, "because I feel like you and I have been through so much over these years, and I've seen you grow . . ."

And then I was crying near the entrance to the staff room, saying, "Oh my gosh!"

Dr. Brown added, "That's only if you want it! You don't have to say yes. That's totally fine. Take some time to think about it and you can let me kn—" I hugged her, and we began laughing and crying, in a good, happy way.

A week later, after I finished my last high school exam in her classroom, she pulled me out into the hall and gave me the first and only quilt I've ever had that was in fact green, green.

I guess green's not too bad.

CHAPTER 14

IT'S OKAY THAT THINGS AREN'T PERFECT

trust yourself

*i thought things would make more sense
when i became an adult.
i thought i'd uncover all of the secrets
that i've always wanted to know,
and all of the secrets that it seemed
everyone else,
or at least every adult, was in on.*

*it turns out, it was the opposite.
growing up i realized that
all of the things
that didn't make sense to me,
actually don't make sense.*

RESEARCHED UNIVERSITIES AS PART OF A PROJECT IN GRADE TEN. I was very thankful this was a project and not something I navigated on my own, because I had no idea how universities—or life after high school, really—worked.

I didn't know what I wanted to be when I grew up. I found it very difficult to imagine my future. Although I was doing better in some areas, like standing up for myself and telling people that I was autistic, I didn't plan on being alive to make those choices, so I'd never thought of them for real before.

I wrote a list of things that I was good at, things that were easier for me to learn and came to me quickly:

- Crocheting
- Solving for x
- Public speaking
- Driving (scary, but easy)
- Knitting
- Teaching
- Data entry
- Dancing
- Making paper cranes
- Singing
- Acting
- Cooking
- Shooting a gun and archery
- Gardening

While I loved to sing and act and dance, and I was good at those activities, I never thought to consider them for jobs when I got older. I was happy to keep them as hobbies with no pressure or obligation. As I looked through the list, I wondered what I could do with skills like shooting a bow and arrow. Unless I planned to be Katniss Everdeen, that wasn't a career option.

Next, I listed things that I found hard to do:

- Basketball
- Soccer
- Baseball
- Dodgeball
- Volleyball
- Tennis
- Staying alive

Then I wrote a list of what I liked:

- I like kids.
- I like anatomy! Anatomy was how I connected with myself. I knew what happened inside me, which made me feel better about the fact that it all went on without my knowledge and my control.
- I was really good at school and very comfortable with studying for a long time.

The more I thought about it, the more I settled on the idea that anatomy was the one subject I really could learn about forever. I'd been studying anatomy since I was a little kid and never got bored. I'd never run out of questions and never had enough answers. It excited me. I decided to go for kinesiology, because whatever I wanted to be when I grew up could go in a different direction after four years, and an anatomy undergrad was probably a pretty solid base for whatever that was.

I chose my university based off distance from home, how reputable the kinesiology program was, how the dorms looked, how easy the website was to navigate, school colors, school name, and overall vibe of the university. McMaster it was.

FIELD NOTES

It turns out, the answer to "why do people do that?" is because they think that's what they're supposed to do. Everyone here is trying, just like I am. No one here knows what they're doing.

I thought when I became an adult, I'd have all of the answers, but becoming an adult is realizing that no one has the answers. We are just the blind leading the blind, trying to help each other and ourselves out as much as we can while trying to understand who we are and who we want to be.

I waited for university to be the best time of my life. High school was a bust overall, but university meant I was going to make so many new first impressions. This time it would be more as myself, as Paige who was autistic. I was going to be surrounded by smart people who were interested in the same things I was, and who cared about school as much as I did. I thought I was going to make so many friends.

I made some, like my roommates. But I found it hard to meet new people when everyone seemed somehow to have friend groups already. It's scary to be a single person walking up to a crowd who already like each other, who are already connecting and laughing and mirroring each other's body language.

FIELD NOTES

I wonder if people do that as a safety mechanism. They find small groups within crowds of people they don't know, and those become their friends.

I can't do that. It's not authentic.

I'd been looking forward to the independence and introducing myself to new people. But as my university life began, I hit a wall everywhere I went. Still, I took step after step. I was patient with myself, even as I was frustrated that my picture of university life wasn't matching reality.

A meal plan was mandatory for all first-year students. This was a card specifically loaded with money to use for food on campus. There were multiple cafeterias and kiosks and restaurants littering campus, and a few in the surrounding area also accepted meal cards for payment. The choice was overwhelming. I thought of Little Paige, with a lunchbox and a bologna sandwich. She would have been terrified by all this choice.

But I could do this.

One step at a time.

One breath at a time.

I still didn't have anyone to sit with in biology.

Not yet.

Being on my own was lonely, but it was also exciting and freeing, all at once. I didn't have a plan. I just went and studied and walked and slept, and I didn't buy groceries for myself and I didn't go to parties. I didn't know how to study or where. Often I didn't know if I wanted to be alive in a year still, and it didn't make sense to me to spend my days stressing about a future I couldn't be sure existed. I just wanted it to work, and for life to have a plan, and to be fine. But any time I stopped and thought about it, I realized there was nothing there. I didn't plan to have anything to look forward to. I never planned to be alive so long. How could I worry about the future when I struggled so much in the present and wasn't sure if there would be a future?

I signed up to be in the university musical that year: *Company*, by Stephen Sondheim. I was trying to want to be alive. I decided to fake it, hoping I would make it, and what better place than onstage?

I played Sarah, and I had an amazing time. The people in theater felt like friends. I started to find people who I vibed with.

I twisted my ankle onstage during our third show and sang off-stage for the next seven shows. I was so sad! But I loved my time spent with the musical. I realized that I made a few great friends. I did well in school, and I liked most of the material, which made it even easier. School was fast, but so was I.

University still felt really hard. I hated going to class and navigating so many people trapped in a big, crowded room. I thought getting a service dog made sense for me and where I was mentally at the time. I got a puppy right after I finished the first year of university. I chose a German shepherd. At eight weeks old, Macey, who's black and red, joined my life. I thought that if I trained her as a service dog, she'd make my life easier, but after a year in training I realized I'd rather just have her be a really good dog. My job has become making her life exactly as she needs. I like looking after her. I love kissing her little wolf face, and I love how her barks sound like she's talking. I like when she jumps up onto my bed. She sleeps with me sometimes.

She's perfect.

I completed my first year of my undergraduate degree with the intention of finishing and pursuing god knows what afterward. One cool thing about kinesiology was I had plenty of options after undergrad. I could specialize wherever I wanted with regards to science and the body, or even just use my undergraduate degree to apply for teachers' college. Teachers' college is a general term for a post-undergrad program to get a bachelor's of education, like applying to law school. Most people who know they want to be teachers out of high school take Concurrent Ed., which combines a four-year undergrad degree with the two years of teachers' college into five years of schooling. I would have to take six, because kinesiology was four years and that's what I started with. I didn't like that necessarily. I also didn't like that my main credentials for teaching, due to my kinesiology degree, were gym and sports related. Maybe I could be a gnarly gym teacher, but for grade ones.

Being a teacher has always been a basic, fallback option for me. The common denominator of who I am and what I like to do and what I'm good at is teaching. This is something I could write on a sticky note now. But I didn't want to teach gym.

My big feelings and my difficulties with figuring out how to stay alive persisted. I decided to reach out for counseling and support. I never had luck with any of that before, but perhaps this time it would be different. Better.

I will find my groove.

At this point, I started dating the older guy again. The one who'd made me hit my head in the car. That guy. My life was continually two good steps, more bad steps. It seemed to me, the summer I turned nineteen, that he'd grown up a lot. I was around him for a few months and was really intrigued and impressed at the person he'd become over the years. He wasn't perfect by any means, but he was so *fun*. He was less angry and more free. I think that's what's supposed to happen as you age and as you get your heart broken. I was proud of him. And he *was* my best friend at one point.

He didn't want to date me then. He didn't want to be in a relationship at all, because he knew he became all-consuming in them, and he had other goals to focus on. He really wanted to save for a house.

When I like someone, everyone else in the world disappears, and I just couldn't leave him alone. We began dating again, although I was hours away in my second year of university.

At this time, I got big into learning about the farming industry and decided to become vegan. I wanted to love being vegan, but because I don't feel hunger very well and because eating enough with zero animal products is difficult in and of itself, I lost a lot of weight quickly. I became very unhealthy. I was exhausted all the time and very small. I knew I needed to eat meat again to survive because of all my food challenges and restrictions. It's still so hard, though. Animal products still make me want to throw up, but I have to eat. Food is a challenge I constantly have to face.

I trained Macey all summer and brought her to school with me in the fall. I rented a house with four others: a first-year roommate, a girl I met in class, her friend, and a random girl our age who we found online. The landlords didn't like Macey there, which I didn't care about, because she was a service dog in training. Macey was still a puppy with tons of energy. Having her around in public stressed me out more than it relieved stress.

After I reached out for counseling and support, I got the university's equivalent of an IEP at the beginning of my second year. I had no idea I could have supports in university as well, or I would've gotten them my first year. It wasn't called an IEP in uni. It was called SAS (student accessibility services). They had an SAS location on campus with a team of fifteen or so people all working on accommodations. I had two counselors working with me on mine, and I had two therapists on the team as well.

I began attending weekly therapy sessions. Yet again, these weren't a good fit for me. During one appointment with my therapist in second year, she walked me down to the hospital attached to the university because she said I was "in danger of hurting myself" and she wanted me in the hospital to keep me safe. I don't even know what I said that ticked her off. I didn't think I spoke differently at that appointment. It was like any other day in therapy, I thought.

I was too exhausted to fight hard. I begged her not to make me go, but she persisted.

"Please don't. Nothing good ever happens in hospitals for me," I said.

"Where else should you be? Where's a better place for you?"

The psychiatrist on call asked the same questions I heard before: "Do you have a plan?"

I tried to bypass answering the questions by getting to the point.

A lot of doctors don't like that because they don't like to be interrupted in their protocol. This psychiatrist was very annoyed by me, I could tell. No part of her face moved besides her mouth and her eyes, which darted from mine to the paper in front of her. She didn't have a lot of sympathy for me, but I was never looking for sympathy. They wanted me to stay the night, but I was only there for six hours. She made me realize it wasn't productive to be attending school when I was also struggling so much with just the living day-to-day stuff. It was late when I left and my mind was broken, but I kept putting one foot in front of the other.

I dropped out of university the next day. I never saw that coming in a million years. I moved home, but the aim was to move out of my parents' house as quickly as possible. I don't talk about my dad often, and that's for reasons maybe I'll share another day, but that summer back home made it clear I didn't want to be there. I needed to make money to do that. I could be quite good as an eyelash technician, or someone who applies lash extensions. I got my lashes done at the time, and I had for a while. The girl who did mine told me more, and it sounded like a really good, safe routine for me. I took a three-day course. In Ontario, there's no need to qualify to do this work—any Joe Blow can say they're a lash tech—but I needed to feel confident in myself before I dared touch another human body.

At my parents' house, the spare room was downstairs, and it was carpeted. Both weren't optimal, health-and-safety-wise, for a lash studio. The spare room was smaller than my bedroom upstairs, but I decided to move my room downstairs so I could renovate upstairs into my lash room.

Graham volunteered to go downstairs instead. "Can I?" he asked. He was sixteen and excited to have the little bit of freedom that came from sleeping on a separate floor from the rest of us. I immediately began working. I was nineteen.

And a few months later was March of 2020. My business stopped and my life stopped, and I found myself spending a lot of time on an app called TikTok.

The internet is a vast, confusing space where everything and nothing happens or is happening and has happened at the same time. Everyone is there and yet no one is there. Anyone could say anything that they want to on TikTok.

I didn't like when people were wrong.

Around this time, there was a video going around that used a "stitch" sound. People would use the sound and then lip-synch the words to make it seem like they said them, and it was funny because it was in a different context than the original usage of the words.

This sound was about autism.

The sound was used in a joking way. People who made videos with the sound made the joke that they were autistic because they had messed up, or were bad at something, or were really dumb and had no idea what was going on.

Funny joke.

I clicked on the sound to see how many videos had been made under it. The sound was becoming a trend; millions of people were making videos.

Millions of people made jokes that they were autistic because they did something dumb, including people I really liked and respected for their advocacy and social justice work.

I started making a little video in my bathroom, recording on my phone to let off some steam. It was true, and it was informative, and so I posted it. I didn't think anyone was really going to see it. In the video, I talked about the sound that was going around and the joke that seemed to be trending. I explained my frustration because the idea that autistic people are stupid is incorrect—it's a stereotype that's ableist and unfair. I based this solely on the fact that I am autistic, and I'm a pretty smart cookie.

People watched this video and were shocked at some of the things I said. It was the first time that a lot of them had heard someone talk about their own autism, I think.

A lot of people didn't believe that I was autistic.

Suddenly it was out in the open. I went from only a few people in my hometown knowing to what felt like the whole world finding out at once. Some people were supportive, but more people, it seemed, were ignorant and rude. I was showered in hateful comments, which really upset me. I was called every name in the book, criticized, and ridiculed for what I said and for what I was doing. When comments were left telling me I was wrong and I was awful, I believed them and wanted to make it better every single time.

I got a lot of people saying variations on "You're autistic, huh? You don't seem autistic."

What I saw as stupidity really bothered me. It frustrated me. So as not to feel crushed by it, I responded. I was powerless if I couldn't teach people and change their minds.

My response was to make more videos
- Giving people facts.
- Telling people about my life.

- Correcting their mistakes.
- Just like Paige with her hand up at school, I had a need to clarify.
- I replied.
- I responded. Again. And again.
- I believe that most conflicts can be solved with education and knowledge. I thought that those commenters would feel differently if they actually understood, so I tried to make them understand.

I think I made a lot of people understand; as time went by, most of the comments became kind and meaningful. Momentum gathered. I made videos that went with the trends. I replied, trying to please. Learned more, responded to people. Suddenly I was up to posting multiple times a day and signed a contract saying I would post at *least* five videos a week, for eight weeks, making at least forty videos TikTok could use for advertising purposes. This deal was signed through a TikTok agent who was assigned to me. It wasn't paid at all: the project was for TikTok to showcase educational content, and they reached out to me.

I scrolled through the main page, collecting ideas. I archived songs and effects and all kinds of videos that I wanted to recreate in my own way. I could understand how to do this job; it involved seeing what other people were doing and recreating that myself. I'd done that my whole life. Now, I could see which videos were popular, which meant those tools would help make my videos popular, too, helping people learn about autism and my experiences.

I bought myself a house with money that I earned over the years. I'd been a secretary for my mom at her office throughout high school. I was a hostess and then a server at a restaurant in town. I tutored high school students in math and science. I acted in a few commercials. I was a teacher's assistant in an anatomy lab in university. I didn't spend; I saved. I collected money from my swear jar. All of that built up over the years, and with the extra money from the lash studio, I paid for my house myself at twenty years old. My house is in the same town, so the huge change could be less of a change, and I'd be near my friends and family. It's a cute, basic bungalow with a good-size yard for being in town, a separate entrance for my lash clients, and a pretty gnarly walk-in closet.

I was suddenly adulting hard and fast: I had a house, like four jobs, a gorgeous dog, and a million eyes on me. It became a lot of work. People stopped viewing me as a human being and started viewing me as a commodity. My worth became based on what service I could provide for others, how much others liked me and agreed with me, and how well I played the game—balancing everyone socially and being individual enough to be interesting but not so much as to rock the boat.

It never felt right to me. Yet at the same time, I found I was connecting in a good way with followers and people online. I loved feeling like I was making a difference. But I started to lose all that.

In the midst of my internet journey, I forgot what I wanted to do, which was be my authentic self. Living my life on social media in accordance with a whole different population that I never experienced before had me forgetting myself all over again.

I'd only just started to figure out who I was and then got jumbled out of fear. Whichever way I stepped, I seemed to run into the next level of my self-development, forcefully.

I kept betraying myself and the values I was creating. I let people get into my head and let their opinions alter my own perception of myself. I realized I felt like I was on fire all of the time, and I didn't want to be on fire anymore.

Mom and I talked to Dr. Hallix. I asked for support for what I thought might be ADHD. And I asked for a psychiatrist. I was doing better at asking for what I needed.

The doctor said that I already had a psychiatrist: the guy who gave me meds when I was taken in that night Mom thought I was going to kill myself.

That guy.

So, Mom reached out to that psychiatrist and we made a phone appointment. The phone call was only about fifteen minutes, but during it, the psychiatrist referred me into a sort of therapy class and prescribed Vyvanse, which is a medication for ADHD. The classes were run by the hospital in town for members of the public (based on a hierarchy, after psychiatric recommendation) to take on depression, anxiety, emotional regulation, self-love, self-worth, and more. Talented nurses at the same hospital where I'd been committed shared their knowledge and experience running the classes and shared a booklet with a hundred pages of information to follow along and learn as they taught. It wasn't supposed to be like group therapy, where the majority of the conversation came from the participants. It was like a classroom. Each class went for a week and was only a few hours a day. I ended up taking two classes a week, for five weeks, so ten courses overall.

I hated talking about my problems. I don't have an issue with opening up or sharing intimate details about myself or anything like that, but I hated how therapists seldom had anything helpful to share back with me. I couldn't help but feel unintentionally exploited by it all. I could have spent the same two hours with a teddy bear and had the same conversation for free. When people say therapy, I think most of them are referring to a particular type of practice that doesn't really work for me. Therapy, to me, is not talking to someone about my problems. I don't need to tell people what I go through or how I feel individually. Some people feel better just if they get to talk about stuff, but I want to solve problems, not just bring them up. And I can solve a lot of problems on my own, but it's really difficult when I can't, and that's what I want help with.

I almost didn't take the depression class because I didn't believe myself to be depressed. Sure, I was diagnosed with depression, but I genuinely thought the only reason I was diagnosed with it was because I kept trying to kill myself. It turns out that class was the most life-changing.

In the first three weeks of the group classes, I learned more about myself with regards to my emotions and my thoughts than over the previous twenty-one years of my life put together. I was really glad I took the course.

On our first day in the class, we wrote down what depression was. We took ten minutes, not talking to anyone else. That was a very difficult exercise for me because I wanted to write down the factual definition of depression. But by doing it separately, everyone had to write down what depression was to them. That's a matter of opinion and not rooted in fact, so there were no "right" answers. That was stressful, but I tried to accept it. I wrote what depression usually looked like to me.

Depression

- Suicidality can go from zero to one hundred if there's a panic attack.
- I have very little capacity to persevere. A small problem can occur and it is kind of just a confirmation that ending my life is the correct thing to do.
- Things that usually brought me joy don't bring me joy even if I search for joy and I try really hard to find joy, which can make me even more upset.

Some things other people wrote down

- Feeling like a burden
- Loss of appetite or excessively eating
- Feeling alone, isolated, and numb

- Throwing up
- A lack of sleep or an excessive amount of sleep
- Feeling like life is happening all around you and you are just an observer, not actively participating
- Physical pain—headaches, back pain, stomachaches
- Avoiding responsibilities
- Failing relationships
- Risk-taking behavior
- Low libido
- More of a need to control
- Feeling that everything is hard or a lot of effort

We learned that all of these things are part of depression rather than a part of you, and that distinction is important. I noted the way the body reacts to what we do not consciously process.

Our next exercise was to write down things that we've done to try to not be depressed. I wrote about going to a psych ward and getting medication. Other people said going for a walk, playing with their dog, getting drunk. We were then asked to look at our coping habits: Did they work? Did they cure your depression? Have you ever not felt depressed after doing those things?

> I thought, *I really hope they all say it didn't work for them, because if it did, these people are fine and I need to leave this class.* But of course, they said no, their depression didn't go away. We laughed about people who suggested yoga or a bubble bath when we were upset. I brought up Dr. Sharon making me do yoga on the floor.
>
> Everyone on the Zoom call chuckled.

Acceptance and commitment therapy (ACT) is designed to help practice accepting your thoughts and emotions without trying to change them.

We've been conditioned to determine whether an emotion is a good or a bad one before we allow ourselves to feel it. People see anger as bad, sadness as bad, depression as bad, and we shouldn't feel those. We should only feel joy at all times! We've been conditioned that when we feel the bad emotions, we need to get rid of them, push them away so we don't feel them anymore and then everything is okay, life is good.

Every day of the group we started with a five-minute mindfulness activity—basically, meditating. I started meditating in yoga when I was ten, but I only started to feel good at it now.

It's easy to feel shame and to feel like you fail at meditating if you have thoughts. It's impossible to keep my mind from wandering. I can't stay in the moment 100 percent of the time. But I learned that in meditation *there is no right way*; there is only practice. I'm pretty sure that meditating is just practicing not having thoughts, and the more you practice, the larger the space in between the thoughts gets. When the mind wanders, try not to stick to any particular thought. Try your best not to judge the thought. Just let it pass.

ACT suggests that part of the battle with depression is actually the suffering we inflict on ourselves by battling with the emotion, which is so counterproductive. As a human person, emotions are meant to exist and be experienced. Emotions are like a little version of you inside your body that has big feelings and needs to tell you what they are.

If I ignore little-kid Paige and tell her to shut up and go away, she's gonna feel all those big emotions, but just by herself. Whereas if I respond to Little Paige with, "Okay, I hear what you're saying and that is a valid thing. Thank you for letting me know," then Little Paige feels heard. My emotions are like that. By listening to them, they move on and I am okay.

We were directed to imagine playing tug-of-war over a large chasm, and on the other side is something that you're battling. Shame, loss, anger, disgust, regret, pain.

Stuck
Imagine you're pulling,
trying to get the other one
to fall into the chasm
pulling constantly,
struggling constantly,
wishing that you could win.

ACT suggests that depression is being in that stuck state. You are using your resources, your energy, and your effort battling something that you will not win, instead of living life prioritizing what you value. Those emotions can also exist while you expend your resources elsewhere.

In order to understand that, you need to understand what you value and how your values should influence your actions, decisions, and relationships.

So naturally, I needed to make a list of what I valued.

What I value
- Truth and authenticity
- Knowledge, intelligence, and eagerness to learn
- Openness and listening to all opinions
- Being direct, not running from confrontation
- Knowing myself and my limits
- Being connected to my body and mind
- Boundaries and self-respect
- Justice, pacifism
- Time alone
- Emotional maturity
- Validating my emotions and my mental state

ACT wants us to let go of the rope and stop battling, stop playing tug-of-war. What if you just let go of the rope? That doesn't mean that the emotion isn't there anymore. It's there over the chasm, but you're not fighting anymore. You're not stuck in one place. You can move around. You can go over here, over there, as fast or slow as you want. You can go far from the emotion, you can come back to it, and you can make choices that are more in line with what you value. There are no good and no bad emotions. We don't need to fight to get rid of an emotion. I used to get upset that I had big feelings, which would make the feelings even bigger. I ruminated and panicked, then thought, *This is bad that I'm having a panic attack*, which made it worse, and so it snowballed.

Now I sit on the edge of the chasm, and I look at my emotions.

Accept them.

Love them.

Let them go.

Set them free.

Now this is not me suggesting that you let go of the emotion and *not feel it*. But what I learned is that an emotion is going to shine through you as long as it exists, and it won't go away if you fight. *It only goes away when you experience it.*

Experiencing it is hard; that's why we try to fight it. But emotions are normal and meant to be felt. When I stopped fighting my emotions, I became very emotional. I felt sadness, anxiety, fear, and I let all of that happen.

I have a picture of me when I was a kid, and I keep it in my room. I look at this picture sometimes and I listen to that little girl and her big emotions. I comfort myself. After a few minutes, the emotions pass.

And I feel so much better
Pain is inevitable
but suffering comes
from prolonging the pain.
What would happen
if you just accepted it,

and you listened to your body

telling you when you felt it?

The final thing that I wanted to talk about, and this one may be my favorite, is cognitive diffusion. It's this whole idea that you don't create your thoughts but often fuse with your thoughts, regardless of their accuracy.

We are not our thoughts.

We can manually control our thoughts like we can our breathing, but as we function as human people, our brain generates thoughts without thought, to interpret the world around us. We bring our biases into those interpretations, and it's very hard sometimes to separate from the thought and remember that *it's an interpretation*. Most of us fuse with 100 percent of our thoughts, meaning that because we have the thought, we think it's correct.

You only want to fuse with thoughts that are workable and that make sense with what you value.

Until that realization, I thought my thoughts were me, a derivative of me. Part of my OCD is intrusive thoughts, and for the last twenty-one years my intrusive thoughts constantly tried to make me believe that I was the worst human being on the Earth. Now I was able to take a step back. My thoughts are not me—my actions are.

Let me give you an example of an exercise we did for this. I'm going to give you three numbers: one, two, three. Now, for the next minute, don't think of those numbers at all.

So, I sat there trying to not think of those numbers. I kept going, "Five, five, five, five, five," and seeing the number five in my brain, to purposely try to *not* think about one, two, or three. But seven times I thought of the numbers one, two, or three. Seven times. I couldn't help it.

My intrusive thoughts will always be there. I don't control them, and I'm no longer judging or blaming myself for having them because I don't deserve that.

I imagine that my intrusive thoughts are something else. Sometimes I name them. "Okay, Brenda!" I say. "Brenda, babe. That's enough."

For me, what this looks like is arguing with Brenda when she's talking trash.

"Paige," she maybe says. "Cut your finger off! Now."

"That's a thought, Brenda, babe," I reply. "Have a nap."

Thoughts
when a thought comes
sit with it
and ask if it's true

listening to the thought
ask
is that thought a part of me?
does that thought
have to influence
my behavior?

wait and breathe
let it pass

CHAPTER 15
THE EAT PRAY LOVE STAGE

little me

i run my fingers over her sharp edges.
"don't they hurt you?" she asks,
in her little voice.
"no, they don't," i reply.

"you gave me such strong hands
your edges aren't sharp to me.
i was made to run my fingers over the hard parts of you,
and i will hold the most painful parts of you

for as long as you need—"
i don't know if it's my voice,
or my calloused hands,
but she becomes softer.

BECOMING A SOCIAL MEDIA WHATEVER-THE-HECK SO QUICKLY didn't agree with me as easily as it did my following. The sudden spotlight was too bright for my autistic eyes, and this is only half a metaphor. It's not particularly calming to have millions of people want to talk to you so suddenly, including in public, personally. I also really struggled with the hate coming at me online, because it really got to my head and bothered me. I cared what those usernames had to say under my posts, and I cared about what videos so-and-so made critiquing my attitude and my opinion and my appearance. I cared and I changed, and I panicked and I practically begged the internet, *What do you want me to be? What the heck am I supposed to be here?*

I had no confidence in myself or my actions and, like when I was at school, I trusted that everyone else knew what to do, so I tried to follow along. I went right back to people-pleasing. I'd managed to come so far and I guess the universe decided I needed to face another challenge.

As time went by, and I learned how to pay attention to my feelings, I realized I didn't need to worry about the "rules" of being an influencer. I didn't need to worry about being the kind of Paige other people wanted me to be. In my mind, I returned to that conversation with Graham in the hallway: *Why do I care about pleasing people who I don't like?* I came back to questions from lessons I learned in class: *What do I value? What matters to me?*

I significantly limited my posting and never checked comments for about a year or so. I took a minute. I wrote lists of what was important to me. I felt like I was following my truth; I was teaching, I was helping kids, it should have made sense and made me happy, but it still didn't feel good. I began reading comments again once I felt like I couldn't give less of a shit what anyone thought of me. Helping people is what drives me, and interacting with fans and speaking to them directly is something I need to do to feel fulfilled with my work online.

As much as I am so appreciative of people who support me on social media, I don't crave their attention or their approval anymore.

So, we'll see how that goes. And where I go.

I trust myself and my actions, and I trust that my intentions are kind and pure.

My biggest pieces of life advice follow.

ONE: KNOW WHO YOU ARE. NEVER STOP LEARNING ABOUT YOU.

The more you know about yourself, the better and more tailored decisions you can make, and the better you'll feel about them. Knowing yourself is the precursor to living any kind of life that matters to you. We all make stupid decisions. That's just part of life. I know I've made some pretty stupid decisions (you've read about some of them in this book). But I'm happy with my stupid decisions, and I don't regret them—even that older guy, who I broke up with all over again, this time for good. When I look back at that relationship, I learned a lot about what I like, and what I don't. I came out of that relationship having learned a lot about myself.

Relationships are a mirror.

It's important to have your own opinions. You need to be able to ask yourself questions and *feel* the answer, not just think it. Listen to your gut, as they say. *Actually think about feeling the emotion in your body.* Some emotions feel light and prickly in my chest; some feel more like heavy rocks in my stomach. Work to sense your emotions and locate them. Sort them. Listen to them. Instead of naming an emotion "worry," "fear," or "despair," I like to name them by what they motivate me to do.

If I say, "This feeling is worry," I notice that makes me feel panic. Instead, I remind myself that humans were not meant to be labeled and put in boxes, because we are so much more complex than that can allow, especially with our emotions. I also remind myself that my emotional experience is different from someone else's *and* different from how mine will ever be again, so it's okay if I don't know what the exact blend of nuanced feelings are called.

Emotions motivate me to:

- Protect myself
- Get closer
- Take control
- Hide
- Open up
- Solve a problem
- Jump in
- Share
- Leave
- And so much more

That's the important information that comes from listening to the emotions in your body.

It's hard to feel that brain–body connection when you're autistic. As it is, I don't feel it when I have to go to the bathroom, or when it's cold enough for a coat. How the heck can I actually "feel" an emotion? How am I supposed to "feel" happy? What does happy "feel" like? *But I know when my body is happy* because I smile. I speak in silly voices. I want to play with Macey. Those little things are important parts of you.

TWO: KNOW WHERE YOU END, AND SOMEONE ELSE BEGINS

Boundaries, baby. You can't know where you end if you don't know yourself, first of all, so that's why this is number two. Once you know what you value and what you need, you can begin to draw the line between you and other people, emotionally and mentally. It's not your job to teach others how to be any kind of way; it *is*, however, your job to teach others how they're allowed to treat you. We do this, whether or not we're aware of it.

You can't change other people, I promise you. And it's actually an intrusion of someone's boundaries to try. They deserve to live their own authentic life and not the life that's perfect for you that you've imagined in your head. People are going to live their own lives and be responsible for their own self-discovery and healing. I used to think: *But if they healed themselves, they'd get better, and therefore be nice to me and treat me the way I want, and then I'd be safe.* Of course. But what're you going to do? Teach everybody? Change everyone's minds? That's way too much stress and responsibility.

People reflect when they want to, not when you want them to. There is nothing you can say to convince someone who doesn't want to be convinced. The only way you can get someone to change is by changing *yourself.*

Know the boundary between other's thoughts and your own. *What other people think about you is none of your business.* People are allowed the privacy of their own thoughts. You can't read minds, and this is a good thing, because it gives you freedom to be delusional about what others think. You cannot possibly know, and so you get to just make it up and believe whatever you want. If relationships are a mirror, whatever you think the other person is thinking about you is just how you think of yourself, anyway. Remember that next time you catch yourself judging someone or attracting the same kind of partners.

Remember your responsibilities and capabilities as a person. Let others be responsible and capable too. That's one of your responsibilities.

I watched my mom (and a lot of other moms) take on many more responsibilities than were hers to handle, with a smile on her face. She never executed any responsibility half-heartedly or with a mediocre outcome. I watched as she spread herself thin trying to do everything and please everyone, and I thought I was supposed to do the same thing. But you don't realize as a kid that your parents aren't normal or perfect. Some kids find out sooner than others; some parents are shittier than other parents.

You are the holder of your own time (for the most part, unless you have kids). If you're stressed about how much work you have to do or how many projects you have on the go, you could probably benefit from doing less. If you are a talented, ambitious, inspired person, there will always be something else that you could do and will want to do. The list of potential tasks is endless. You are just physically incapable of doing everything, so if you can't limit yourself, time will. No one else will do it for you.

The people who want to take your mental and emotional energy do not have boundaries for how much they're willing to take, so *you* need to have boundaries on how much you're willing to give.

THREE: STUDYING PSYCHOLOGY IS A DIRECT WAY TO LEARN ABOUT THE INNER WORLD OF A BASIC HUMAN PERSON

A whole field of study is dedicated to understanding the mind and behavior of people. That means there are a heck of a lot of resources for you to look at to learn about how people communicate and view the world. You'll accidentally learn a bit about yourself too.

The more you understand psychology, the more you will uncover about your own mind and about the minds of others. It helps you understand how people communicate, and for autistic people like me, it's interesting and a clue to feeling safer in this confusing world.

FOUR: LEARN ABOUT WHAT YOUR CHILDHOOD TAUGHT YOU, HOW YOU INTERPRETED IT, AND WHERE IT SHOWS UP IN YOUR LIFE TODAY

Little Paige learned to exist as best she could, with her limited resources. Now that I'm an adult who doesn't live with her parents, an adult who has her own responsibilities and takes care of herself (how well is irrelevant), Little Paige's responses no longer protect me. She people-pleased and masked and hid her true self and emotions. She kept herself constantly busy and filled with adrenaline and cortisol and didn't believe she could ever trust anybody.

She lives in me, and she always will as long as she is hurting.

The human brain is remarkably adaptable, made for evolution and change and prepared to face challenges to gain knowledge and skills accordingly. When the brain perceives threats, it sets the nervous system on fire, asking it to do something to eliminate the threat and be safe. Depending on the patterns of someone's responses, neural pathways are strengthened (full circle, eh?), and eventually, if the nervous system deals with a threat often enough, the response can become automatic and natural. That pathway of reaction can become easy and even happen accidentally when faced with an entirely different threat.

Our brains adapt to help us survive in our environment. This is great when the environment is consistent. But this is where our adaptive trauma brain doesn't live up to the hype. Our brains are not necessarily the best at undoing what they've already done. Once we've changed and adapted, we stay there. And we are there until we put in the work, not to undo it but to redo it with the resources we've gained along the way.

Learning about attachment wounds from childhood has positively impacted my life the most—as in, it has caused the most significant change to my everyday peace. I must access deep, unhealed parts of my inner child and bring them to the surface to deal with them. This continues to be something I practice daily and will never be fully finished with. I question my thoughts a lot. Most of the time, it's to question if they're mine or if they belong to somebody else.

Do you believe that?

Who told you that first?

Who projected themselves onto you, and you absorbed it?

Do you need to hold onto it anymore?

I ask the hard questions. I listen to my body. I revisit those memories that make me want to cry and scream and throw up, and sometimes I do. I sit with the emotion. I sit with Little Paige. I don't tell her she's too big for me to handle or too much for me to listen to.

I hold her and I say, "You seem very upset right now. That does sound like something upsetting. I'm sorry you're upset. You're allowed to be upset here. I will hold you and love you while you cry, for as long as you need. I love you. You have me. I'm so happy you're alive."

I was already perfect. Before anyone told me I wasn't, I was. There is nothing about me that is flawed or wrong. If someone tries to convince you that you're not perfect just the way you are, that's because they're trying to sell you something.

You're not a little kid anymore, but never forget who you were as a child. Don't forget what you loved and what you knew in your heart was true, before anyone made you feel unsafe and convinced you otherwise.

FIVE: RECOGNIZE THE SYSTEMS AND IDEAS SOCIETY IS BASED UPON AND HEAVILY INFLUENCED BY

Systems change the way individuals think. The abstract concept that is *society* and all its constructed glory isn't easy for me to get a hold on. It may make no sense to me why others believe the things they do, but they become a lot more predictable when I understand how societal norms and standards influence their thoughts and behavior.

This is particularly fascinating because some people's brains are not neurodivergent, and they comfortably sit in social norms. What they believe isn't even a second thought, and some find it absurd for you to bring up the possibility that it should be. It's hard for a lot of people to accept a reality that isn't theirs, even when it is someone else's reality. I think people have a hard time with change, too, which is supposed to be an autistic thing, but I don't know anyone more passionate about change than autistic people. We are the ones who change systems.

Learn about the ways that a person's brain can already be programmed when you interact with them. And the subconscious thoughts *you* might have accidentally absorbed because society told you so. It'll make you feel safe and more in control in a lot of sectors of your life, and it'll inspire you to take steps toward a future you want.

SIX: IT'S EASIER TO BE AT PEACE WHEN YOU CAN UNDERSTAND EVERYONE'S PERSPECTIVE

When your dog is in the way while you're cooking in the kitchen, is it because your dog is just *that* awful and wants to be in your way? No, but you lashed out because the potatoes were boiling over, and you were going to have to clean a big mess on the stove, which stressed you out and made you yell at your dog for being in the way.

You didn't have to yell. You could have gone around your dog, or asked them to move, or put them away in their crate while you cooked to avoid this in the first place.

My dog just wants to be beside me all day, because that's what dogs do. Macey loves being close to me and being involved in whatever I'm doing. She likes it when I give her a job to do, and if I don't, her job becomes whatever I'm doing. And when I see it like that, I don't want to yell at her. I want to kiss her face and say, "I love you too!"

It's not her fault she's a German shepherd and I have a small kitchen. I'm grateful to have a dog who loves me so much that she wants to stand next to me while I'm being boring, cooking potatoes. It's my job to nourish her, which includes teaching her to respect my boundaries and caring for her so she trusts me and listens to me. Mace has a mat she goes to lay on while I cook, far away from the stove.

Everything you do is a projection of you.

The same goes for everyone else.

SEVEN: YOU HAVE TO ACCEPT WHATEVER YOU CAN'T CHANGE

No amount of thought, stress, or worry can change the fact that you are not in control of an outcome. I'm not saying, "So just don't stress!" But I am saying this as cold, hard truth and also hopefully as reassurance.

Because this is what ends up reassuring me.

Worrying about something in the future that may or may not even happen is an unusable worry, because if that thing does actually happen, then you'll worry again for a second time. If it doesn't happen—which is most of the time, to be honest—then you just worried for nothing. You can't control what you worry about, but you can work on focusing on different, more productive, and more accurate thoughts about your worry.

I used to be terrified of flying on an airplane. I was afraid any flight I was on would crash, and my survival would be in the hands of incompetent strangers who didn't know me and there would be absolutely nothing I could do to save myself. That fear was paralyzing on my first airplane ride. Now I'm confident on a plane because the only other choice is to be stressed on a plane, and the latter is less fun. (And now I have the tools to be able to make that choice.)

The likelihood of my flight crashing doesn't change whether I worry about it or not. I can stress the most in the whole world, harder than I've ever stressed before, and that stress still cannot fly a plane properly. No amount of stress can supernaturally save me.

If my plane is going to crash, then it's going to crash.

Worrying about my lack of control over an outcome doesn't give me more control, and ruminating over my helplessness isn't productive. Yes, it's scary. It's also probably going to be okay. And even if it isn't, I trust my abilities to get myself through it as best as I can.

You can't always avoid the bad stuff. You've gotta trust yourself. You have to trust that you're capable of handling it.

Feel your feelings, but remember the facts behind your feelings. Your feelings aren't fact.

Stress and worry usually tell us to change something. It motivates us to take immediate action. When there's no immediate action to take, that's when I remind my worry, my Little Paige, that her worry does not serve me anymore. There is no action to take, and she can settle and be a kid.

Change is inevitable, life is unexpected, your plans are often wrong, and you cannot control it at all.

I choose to let go of what I cannot control and focus on what I can.

Which is really just my actions.

EIGHT: NOTHING MEANS ANYTHING UNTIL YOU MAKE IT MEAN SOMETHING

I didn't know how to be a person, so I studied people. I think everyone tries to learn how to be a person the way they want to be. Some people look to religion. Depending how devoutly someone practices their religion, and how exactly they interpret the text, holy books are like rule books to those devotees. Religion is where some people find meaning.

I am not religious—I don't like labels and boxes—but I am spiritual. I find meaning in the universe and in nature, outside of a societal system.

One

I am the universe, and every change is meant for me.
I take change as it is meant to be and comes
at me, to me, for me.

I don't think that there is meaning in everything. I don't think everything needs to have meaning behind it or any significance at all. It doesn't even have to be important. Some things just . . . are. And that's all. That's all they have to be.

I think that we, as humans, are the meaning. We give our meaning into otherwise meaningless subjects, objects, concepts, and ideas. We decide what is meaningful, from our perspective, through the lens of importance we've created in our lives.

When I was twelve and tasked to find the meaning of a song, I couldn't, because nothing had meaning to me. Meaning wasn't something I cared about because there wasn't a pattern I could depend on to explain it. It isn't conceptual. It's emotional.

Stevie Nicks wrote the lyrics to "Landslide" in one sitting, following a divorce. There's no meaning to a song about divorce to me, even though that's the literal meaning of that song. Now, I find my own meaning. The song gives me a space to reflect on my life, reminding me that everything I love is going to change me.

It's all about perspective. No one can tell you what to find meaningful. That's so exciting, because you can find meaning everywhere once you start nourishing what you love.

NINE: MOST PEOPLE DON'T KNOW WHAT THEY'RE DOING

There's no singular person to blame. We are all people trying our best, each person thinking and feeling like they are doing the best they can (most of the time). All of these traumatized, broken individuals want to live life a little less broken and are doing that in whatever way they think is right. And most of them are so wrong. But they don't know. And if they don't wanna know, they'll never know. And it's not their fault. And it's also not mine.

TEN: IT'S NOT SUPPOSED TO BE PERFECT. IT'S JUST SUPPOSED TO BE.

Once you make that the new rule, it's easier to be okay most of the time.

Perfection doesn't exist.

A lot of people go through life seeming to never be satisfied with their work and their efforts. So, they keep going and keep trying because maybe someday they'll be as rich as they want, or as famous as they want, or as pretty as they want.

I don't know why I felt like someday I could work hard enough to be perfect. That if only I worked hard enough and tried hard enough, someday I wouldn't have to try anymore. But I think I'll always try. I'll always push. And it won't be enough to be perfect. I push and I try, and I do so because *that's who I am*. There's no amount of work or effort I could put in that could be enough for me, and that's amazing. I learned to enjoy where I was, relinquish the idea of control, and stop chasing a perfect calm, a perfect thought, a perfect relationship, world, idea, time.

You'll continue to try. And you'll fail a lot. And you'll let the child within your heart make your adult decisions sometimes. You'll mess up and you'll make mistakes. Sometimes, you can do everything right and it still won't go your own way. Things don't make sense.

But you don't have to be who you used to be. It's not your responsibility to live up to the expectations that other people have made up in their head about you. It's not your responsibility to be perfect. Or to be anything.

You're *human*. You're supposed to make mistakes and create new neural pathways and evolve. Get comfortable in fucking up. Give 70 percent. Give 30 percent sometimes.

There is no end goal. There is no finish line. Today exists. Make choices.

THE DIFFERENCES

When you skin your knee, a lot of processes happen in your body to protect yourself. Before the body even begins to heal the wound, it has to alert the nervous system that something harmful is taking place and needs to stop to prevent further damage. Pain tells us to pay attention. In my experience, physical pain is easier to feel than psychological pain. For most of my life, I didn't know I was in psychological pain. I didn't know the psychological wounds I had were wounds. I thought the hard times I had were because *I* was a hard time—the wound was a core, integral part of my character.

I needed everything to be perfect
Always stressed.
Always crying.
Bossy.
Alone.

Through these last few years on social media, I've learned a lot about autism and myself and the way I feel I'm supposed to fit comfortably in the world. A subcategory of autism that I am currently learning more about is called pathological demand avoidance (PDA). A lot of people in the community call it "persistent drive for autonomy," which helps explain it clearly. It's not about defying others; it's about needing complete autonomy, however that might look. Autistics with PDA have their nervous system set on fire *any time there is a loss of autonomy*. The PDAer is threatened any time they feel they're being controlled or a hierarchy feels established. The nervous system has the same reaction to an incoming bear attack as it does when Mom says, "Go brush your teeth." While PDA is something that I am just now learning more about, I want more autistics to look into it. It explains so much about my history.

I bring it up because, basically, Little Paige's nervous system was constantly on fire. The PDA response is different for everyone, depending on how it was responded to throughout childhood. I had to eliminate threats constantly, alone, by myself. I fawned with extensive people-pleasing and no emotional boundaries, fought by arguing and yelling, fled by making an excuse or dissociating, or froze crying.

I was tiny, with no idea of why, or how, or even where I was on fire all the time.

"You're not on fire!" people metaphorically told me. "We're *all* on fire! Everyone feels this way."

But they were wrong.

FIELD NOTES

I love that I have access to so much of the world that most people don't.

I love how good I am at finding patterns.

I'm a really good teacher because once I understand the student, I know exactly why they aren't understanding something, and I know exactly how to explain it to them or how they should do it that will make it all click.

I love how I'm not held back as much as everyone else is by made-up rules about how much they should care about people they don't even know. I am much more free. I feel like most allistic society is brainwashed in a way by standards they've never even thought to question.

I'm glad I'm autistic so I question the right stuff.

I have very good intuition.

I store every memory.

I love so intensely and so deeply.

My brain is pretty cool.

I love being autistic. I truly do. Every piece that makes me autistic is a piece that I would not trade away.

Life isn't all sunshine and rainbows—in fact, I still have no idea what I'm doing—but that's alright.

Any autism-specific therapy I went to tried to teach me how to give proper eye contact, what social cues mean and how to add them into conversation, how to make friends and to talk to people, how to act properly at a restaurant, and other bullshit that I did not care about at all. I remember looking one therapist in the face, thinking, *You can't be serious. I don't care at all about how much eye contact someone else deems acceptable. Or what kind of clothes are going to get me the most friends. I just want to stop having panic attacks. I want to stop having a billion ping-pong thoughts in my brain. I want to stop wanting to kill myself.*

The problem was that I wasn't *happy*. And I was autistic too.

Vyvanse was an enormous help. I started on ten milligrams and the psychiatrist titrated me up to thirty milligrams per day. Dr. Hallix didn't prescribe it to me because it is a controlled substance, which, like Ativan, can be addictive. I have to show my ID every time I pick up my Vyvanse, and I can only collect it on the exact day that I run out. It's an amphetamine, like a cousin of meth.

I was prepared to feel like Superman as soon as I started taking it.

For the first week taking it, I noticed I was ripping into my to-do lists. Mowing through task after task that usually took me so much planning. Now I was getting up and doing things because I was feeling so good. I wrote more lists to myself, which was easy to do because my brain felt *quiet*, and with that, I had energy. I understood it was eventually going to mellow out and I would not be such a productive machine forever, so I prepared Future Paige with lists. That meant she wouldn't have to think.

In this Superman stage, a friend came to see me in my new house. I was wiping the corners of my kitchen counters, behind the toaster, behind the stove. "Look," she said. "I'm just noticing, and . . ." She paused. "You seem manic."

With the medication, I'm no longer trapped in a situation where everything's happening all at once and I can't focus on one thing.

"I disagree," I replied to my friend, smiling. "It's quite the opposite: I feel calm and focused. I'm okay for the first time." I wiped around where she was sitting. "It's amazing. I get up and just make my bed and clean the kitty litter. I take a shower. I do the dishes. I'm being a human being."

Practical questions for making life easier at home

1. What do I have a hard time doing?
   Example: I have a hard time dealing with mess.
   Now that I know that, I ask more questions:
- Where does mess accumulate?
- Do I leave dirty dishes in the sink for a long time?
- Do I have a lot of dirty laundry regularly? Is the dirty laundry in the hamper or in a pile on the floor?
- Do I make my bed?
- Is my workspace clean?
- What's the inside of my car like?

2. Next, I ask myself, *Why?* This helps me find the obstacles in my way that consciously or subconsciously make each of the tasks difficult to complete.
- The laundry hamper is all the way down the hall. I get out of my dirty clothes in my bedroom, so it's easier to leave them in a pile in the bedroom.
- I have to do the dishes manually and don't like to because they are loud, so I avoid them subconsciously.
- Macey is sitting in front of the dishwasher and I don't wish to disturb her. That's why the dishes are still in the sink.
- There's too much junk in the garage so I have a hard time moving around my car to get clutter out from different seats.

3. I work with myself, not against myself. I see my patterns, so I talk myself through it: *What can you do to make your life easier? Don't be afraid to be unconventional! That's the point. What can you do to make fewer steps? To make completion easier?*
- Have a laundry hamper in the bedroom
- Get bamboo dishes or other dishes that are quieter
- Make sure there isn't a mat in front of the dishwasher or the dog may like to lie there

- Clear out a space in the garage around the car so I can access the seats better to declutter them
4. I remind myself that I don't have to do everything all at once. Doing 10 percent is better than doing 0 percent, whether you believe it or not, Little Paige.
   - Doing some of the dishes
   - Vacuuming the living room
   - Using a lint roller to get crumbs off the bed
   - Writing one sentence
   - Having a bite of food
   - A light jog

Now I think I know my place in this world, on the internet, in relation to others. I know who I am a little bit more every day, and I feel safe. I don't have a community online personally, and it's always been hard to find my crowd. The important thing is I do have some very valuable, important connections in my friends that are authentic and nurture me. We all work and live far apart, though. I'm still pretty solitary, just doing my thing, learning, asking questions, reflecting, and sharing what I can to help others.

And I know at least a smidge about how I wish to navigate the world around me from now on. I want to be here and experience *experiences*, and that's all there needs to be.

Mom and I have become closer over the years, and that's because of boundaries, not in spite of them. Now, as I have my own home, I feel like each conversation we have is very important to her. That makes me feel good. Since that therapy session together, she's dropped so many defenses. She provides such a compassionate ear and desires to do better for me. That unwavering drive feels a lot like what I think love feels like.

I'm content with living now. I'm content with my growth, including every frustration and every failure. When I was growing up, people always said that life was going to get harder. But although life did get harder, I got smarter and stronger. I actually have not wanted to die now for a while.

I still continue to date people, on and off. I never cared to tell anyone I was autistic, really, unless I got really close with the person and wanted to introduce them to ways they could help me in a bad time. Now, people kinda know I'm autistic as soon as I give them my Instagram handle.

The focus always remains on living a life that's authentic to me and being honest in my personal relationships. I try to take care of Little Paige, protecting her, not betraying her boundaries or making her uncomfortable. I listen to what I want and don't want, knowing that will always change.

Still trying to navigate life

Life is not good all the time. I panic. I cry. Things are hard, and there's a lot that I haven't figured out. Life isn't perfect. I'm upset a lot. I'm autistic all the time; I always will be. Making choices is difficult. Making a routine is hard.

But.

I think it's a blessing we're given as humans to have the ability to feel so much and make the mundane capable of sparking joy and excitement. We have such fire in us; we have a drive to be involved and to connect to the world around us. There's a little whimsy in us that creates wondrous events in real life, just because we can. Human thoughts are that powerful. That's so beautiful.

Graham and I are still close. We grew up with very different childhoods, and our parents responded to our needs very differently, and I was always afraid that he wouldn't understand me. He's shown me that you don't need to understand someone fully to care about them and love them. He supports me, and I always feel connected to him. The person my brother is today is still my favorite person in the world. I'm not sure what his future plan is. I don't think he knows either, and I don't think he ever has, so it's business as usual. He's older now than I was when I got big on TikTok; he's working and being an adult.

As a family, we've come to realize that my whole family is neurodivergent. Now that we see *that*, it's easy to understand why we accepted the mess and the upset as normal.

I have a few friends who accept me for who I am. As long as I act in accordance with what's honest and valuable to me, and I make the best choice I can possibly make at the time, then I have no need for regret. If there's nothing I could have done better at the time, then I know I did my best.

Bests
I do it. It goes.
It keeps going.
I keep choosing me
as best as I can.
Most people are trying
their hardest
and doing
what they think is best.
Everyone just
has different "bests."

Macey lays down on the couch in front of the window in the living room. It's draped with that green quilt from Dr. Brown, because that's easier to clean than the couch. But I do love my sleeping ball of fur. As I come to these final thoughts, she looks over at me, hopeful, perhaps, that we'll go into the yard and throw a ball soon. She'll run so fast, and I'll laugh at her silly face. She can jump so high. We could play all day.

I go to sit with her.

I'm pretty sure that being a kid should be one of the easiest and happiest parts of your life. But it isn't for everyone. I learned a lot over the last few years, and I've learned that there's more to come. I notice how every day I'm kinder to myself and my chest feels lighter.

I take one more deep breath.

settle

she has her head in my lap.
as she dreams,
her paws run,
her tail wags.

i wonder
what we're doing
in her dream.

and what we'll do next
in mine.

ACKNOWLEDGMENTS

I want to thank:

- My best friend, Renée, for going to Costco and stocking my fridge for me while I was glued to my desk, writing for weeks. Thank you for keeping me alive and socialized and loved.
- Ms. Dales, for being super dope to me when I was twelve and making me feel safe, heard, and accepted for the first time. For making me feel like I was worth it.
- My brother, Graham, for your compassionate and kind heart. For always having my back.
- Every person who has ever said something negative about me, for pushing me to learn more and more about the person I was.
- Every person who has ever said something positive about me, for helping me create a space of self-worth and a determination to thrive.
- My agent, Emmy, and editor, Mollie, who helped prep me and my story for the world. Thank you both for your patience, wisdom, and guidance as we worked on my first book.
- Alice, for jumping in last minute and being the greatest support and influence I could ask for.

- Everyone on the team at Hachette who worked on making this book come to life; thank you to Monica, Sean, Liz, Amy, Amanda, Lauren, and Kara.
- Finally, I want to thank Little Paige, for not killing herself, for surviving every awful day and creating the life I have now. The flowers are beautiful. I'm glad I'm here.

REFERENCES

American Psychiatric Association, DSM-5 Task Force. *Diagnostic and Statistical Manual of Mental Disorders: DSM-5*. 5th ed. Washington, DC: American Psychiatric Association, 2013.

Sheffer, Edith. *Asperger's Children: The Origins of Autism in Nazi Vienna*. New York: W. W. Norton & Company, 2018.

Tang, Guomei, Kathryn Gudsnuk, Sheng-Han Kuo, Marisa L. Cotrina, Gorazd Rosoklija, Alexander Sosunov, Mark S. Sonders, et al. "Loss of mTOR-Dependent Macroautophagy Causes Autistic-Like Synaptic Pruning Deficits." *Neuron* 83, no. 5 (2014): 1131–1143.